Dancing
with your
Shadow

*Integrating the Ego and the Self
on the Spiritual Path*

Kim Nataraja

MEDIO MEDIA

Scripture texts in this work are taken from the The New English
Bible. Used by permission.

Published by
Medio Media
The Publishing Arm of the World Community for Christian Meditation

Copyright ©2006 by Kim Nataraja

ISBN
978-1-933182-53-7
1-933182-53-9

2006 1st printing United States of America
2007 2nd printing Singapore

Cover design: Carlos Siqueira
Layout and book design: Sharon Nicks

"I would know my shadow and my light so at last I shall be whole"

Michael Tippett
from *Child of Our Time*

Dedicated to the other three dancing Natarajas

Shankar, Shanida and Ramesh

*With gratitude for all the blessings of
your love, nurture and support*

ACKNOWLEDGMENTS

My grateful thanks go to Gene Bebeau and John Wagner for their generosity in sponsoring this book and to Medio Media for publishing it.

My special thanks also go to Laurence Freeman OSB for his encouragement, personal interest and efforts to ensure this book got published.

This book would not have come into being if not for the reactions of participants in Workshops and Seminars over the years. Their requests to put this material in writing, backed by the strong encouragement of my husband, Shankar, my daughter, Shanida, and my son, Ramesh, finally induced me to sit at my computer and start this labour of love.

I also extend my gratitude to them and to other brave friends for reading the first and subsequent drafts, giving me valuable feedback, in particular Laurence Freeman OSB, Angela Greenwood, Jill Rowe, Margaret Lane, Dr. Mark Green, James Yates, and Dini and Sybren Kalkman.

My warm thanks also go to my daughter, Shanida, for her editing and advice and to Sharon Nicks for the careful reading and reformatting of the text prior to printing and whose patience with my alterations is much appreciated.

I also value the time and energy spent by Shirley du Boulay and Rev. Professor Andrew Louth reviewing the book prior to publication and by Carlos Siqueira for creating the humorous illustrations and cover.

Kim Nataraja

CONTENTS

FOREWORD

St Augustine believed that people did not desire happiness enough. He is making a point that we today, still struggling to integrate psychology and religion, could benefit from considering. Our social level of unhappiness and the violence and emotional dysfunction associated with it (and that often flows directly from it) call both for deep religious insight and the psychological awareness of what it is we truly desire.

What so often blocks us is what Kim Nataraja, invoking a rich psychological term, calls the 'shadow'. In this book she speaks from her own experience of the spiritual path and of accompanying others on it, of the art of dancing with the shadow, rather than repressing or fleeing from it in fear. This is necessary for everyone whatever their way of life because what is repressed or feared has a way of taking revenge and asserting itself negatively. It can block creativity, diminish the capacity to love and be loved and so rob life of its joy and brilliance. It is especially important, however, for people with a conscious commitment to spiritual practice or with a religious identity. For them the shadow can loom as a dark counterpoint to the bright ideal they set for themselves or feel drawn to realise.

Kim Nataraja has learned much of what she shares so usefully from her practice of meditation in the Christian tradition. From the teaching of John Main and, through him, back to the roots of the Christian mystical tradition, she can draw both on ancient insights expressed in the language of a great tradition and on contemporary discoveries. In the wisdom of the Christian desert especially, she finds kindred teachers for whom the psyche and the spirit were twin aspects of the process of prayer. Purification, integration and divinisation are universal dimensions of the stages of human development. In these pages the Christian meditator and indeed anyone who has begun to engage with this essential human process will find a guide, a friend and a teacher to walk – and to dance – with.

Laurence Freeman OSB

INTRODUCTION

What is Meditation?

Dancing with Your Shadow deals with the journey of meditation and with what helps and hinders us in practising this discipline.

Meditation is a universal spiritual discipline central to most of the World Religions and Wisdom Traditions. There are many different forms of meditation in these various traditions, all equally valid in their own way. In all the emphasis is on practise and experience rather than theory and knowledge.

It is also an authentic discipline in Christianity, although sometimes it feels that this is the world's best kept secret. Jesus taught contemplation and this way of prayer flourished especially in the 4th century amongst the Desert Fathers and Mothers of Egypt and Palestine. John Cassian collected their teachings in his book *Conferences*. It is in these writings that John Main OSB, a Benedictine monk, re-discovered this tradition for our time and opened it up for all people, calling it Christian meditation. This discipline is now taught by his successor, Laurence Freeman OSB, director of the World Community for Christian Meditation. It is not only the way of prayer of the Desert Fathers and Mothers but also of countless Christian mystics throughout the ages up to our present time.[1]

Meditation is a form of contemplative prayer that leads us into the presence of the Divine beyond thinking and understanding. Rather than talk to the Divine in formal prayers – as we are taught to do from childhood onwards – we let go of words and images and listen to "the small still voice" deep within the silence. Thus we become aware of the Divine within us and there we discover that in our own deep centre we are connected with everything and everybody.

This way of prayer affects all parts of our being: body, mind and spirit. By relaxing the body and letting go of our daily preoccupations, we enter a state of deep relaxation, which has many well-known health benefits. In centering ourselves through meditation we are also more able to deal with the hectic pace of life from a position of balance and harmony. Stilling the body and the mind allows the spiritual side of our being to come to the fore and inform our life.

To help us enter the silence we repeat a prayer word or phrase of spiritual significance: a mantra. By focusing on this mantra we learn over time to let go of our thoughts. The one recommended in the World Community for Christian Meditation is *maranatha*, the most ancient Christian prayer in Aramaic, the language Jesus spoke. We use a word that has little association for us so as not to tempt us into more thought. This is a prayer said with love; it is

---

[1] For further information on the roots of Christian meditation and the role played by John Main and Laurence Freeman please see 'Epilogue'.

not a club to hit our thoughts, but a gentle aid leading to one-pointed attention. It allows us to turn our awareness away from ourselves and all our concerns, fears and hopes. It is a way of breaking through the barrier of self-consciousness into true self-knowledge; in this way we access the power of silence and stillness. The discipline is simple:

Sit down. Sit still and upright. Close your eyes lightly. Sit relaxed but alert. Silently, interiorly begin to say a single word. We recommend the prayer phrase, maranatha. *Listen to it as you say it, gently but continuously. Do not think or imagine anything spiritual or otherwise. If thoughts and images come, these are distractions at the time of meditation, so keep returning to simply saying the word. Meditate twenty to thirty minutes each morning and evening.*[2]

This sounds simple, but it is not easy; yet it is worthwhile. In fact it is "the first task and the first responsibility of each one of us."(John Main)

In the following chapters we will learn practical ways of arriving at stillness of body and mind to make it easier to enter this inner silence of meditation. The main difficulty will be quieting the mind and its chaotic thoughts that seem at first to be never-ending. But we will learn how to minimize and leave them behind.

We will also learn about other possible obstacles that may hinder our meditative practice. We will encounter the wiles of

---

[2] If you are new to meditation you might like to look at this stage of introductory guidance in Appendix II

the *ego* that colour our perception, and we will learn to see through them so that we "cleanse the doors of perceptions and see reality as it is – infinite!" (William Blake)

PROLOGUE

I do not seek to follow in the footsteps of the men of old;
I seek what they sought. – Basho

The spiritual path is a journey of integrating Mind and Heart, the *ego* – our surface personality – and our deeper *self*, which is the centre of our whole being and the link with the Source of All. It is a journey of discovery of the lost and forgotten parts of the totality of our being. As in all adventures there is pain – pain in the remembering why there was loss and the pain of change, of being compelled to leave our comfortable, well-trodden path and forging new paths. But there is also joy – joy in being reunited with forgotten aspects of our soul, and the joy of wholeness and discovering our way home.

Being on the path sometimes feels to be a very isolating and bewildering experience. It is therefore very useful to have a map of the territory. The only reliable map we can have for any trek into the unknown is the one drawn up by those who have travelled that way before, willing to share their experience. In this case the pioneers are the mystics of all Wisdom Traditions. Yet we have to use these maps carefully, always remembering the words: "Believe those who are seeking truth. Doubt those who find it." (André Gide)

Moreover, we all have different starting points, depending on our mind-set and emotional/psychological/social conditioning; the territory seems different depending on our perception, on our own state and level of consciousness.

On my life-long journey there have been guides, people I love and admire, beacons of hope that inspired and gently steered me, sometimes quite unintentionally. These have included inspiring teachers from many different Wisdom Traditions: Jesus, especially the one found in the *Gospel of John* and the *Gospel of Thomas,* Sri Aurobindo, Mother Meera, Paramahansa Yogananda, Bede Griffiths, Lao Tzu, the I Ching, HH The Dalai Lama, Thich Nhat Hanh, John Main and Laurence Freeman. And to these I need to add the authors of many books too numerous to mention. Books that were recommended by friends and strangers, sometimes falling off the shelf in a store or drawing my attention in a library, which was exactly what I needed at that particular time.

My hope is that this book may fulfil that role for you and be a clear map into deeper levels of reality, whichever spiritual practice you are following at present. I will be showing you a map drawn from the Christian Tradition, which is far more mystical than is normally appreciated.

I am like you, an ordinary seeker after truth, looking for meaning, a transpersonal dimension to life, not apart from or transcendent to life but infusing and supporting it, giving meaning to everything we do and are. To quote Mahatma Gandhi: "I claim to be a passionate seeker after truth, which is another name for God."

My own journey has been a spiral one, starting within conventional Western Christianity, then exploring and greatly benefiting from the wisdom of the East: Hinduism, Buddhism, Taoism and Zen, and then coming back home to an understanding of a Christianity that is more spiritual than I would ever have imagined. I went from just sitting still and repeating a phrase from the Lord's Prayer to Indian Mantra meditation, breath/energy control and then back to Christian mantra meditation. All of these disciplines had basically the same effect in focusing the attention and were equally useful in entering the silence of true meditation. My way therefore has always been a contemplative one, of practising meditation, although only in the last thirty years of my life have I been consciously aware of using this discipline.

My background is that I was an only child born in the war and raised between two religions: Catholic and Protestant. This caused a traumatic experience:

It was the commotion, rather than any particular sound that woke me. I was aware of my mother standing next to my bed, pressed against the wall. In the open doorway I saw my paternal grandfather. The next thing that happened was a yelp of fear from our dog, Tilly, as she flew through the air towards my mother. She caught Tilly in her arms. I sat bolt upright in bed. My movement deflected the anger of my grandfather. He looked at me, turned round and left the room. My mother, whilst holding me close, explained that they were arguing about Jesus.

This incident with the dog was caused by an argument between my Protestant mother and her father-in-law, my Catholic grandfather. Waking up from sleep, I felt its effect was traumatic. The world seemed suddenly an insecure and threatening place. It thoroughly shook my view of the adults surrounding me; it made me wary of them. Being a spectator over time to the violence and harm caused by these different interpretations of Scripture made me distrust words about God. It also made me feel alienated from strict denominational religion.

Fortunately this was balanced by an earlier spiritual experience which made me look at ordinary reality in quite a different way. I spent the first four years of my life with my maternal grandfather and grandmother. Their life was an expression of their Christian faith with its simplicity and devotion to service to all who needed it in their small village community. One night I will never forget I was awakened by my grandmother's voice: "Wake up child! Come with me."

My maternal grandmother lifted me out of bed and took me by the hand. We left the house, entered the path running by the house to the cemetery. "Just look!" I was suddenly wide-awake. The whole world was bathed in the unearthly magical light of the full moon, the barn, the house, the trees, and the path. Suddenly there was no sense of self, no looking, just the light. My grandmother's voice, saying, "Come, child!" seemed to come from a distance. She lifted me up and carried me back to bed.

The memory of that *Light* has always saved me from sliding into a negative attitude to life. Instead, my longing for that other reality, glimpsed on that moonlit night, sustained me and created a distance, a detachment from the world in which I found myself. The veil that parts the different realities is not as opaque in early childhood as it later becomes.

Mine was a lonely childhood and as a consequence I had feelings of being rejected, not being of value and not being lovable: false images I had to let go of. Yet at the time this aloneness turned me to an appreciation of nature and of the value of silence and solitude, which fed the contemplative side of my personality. It shaped in me a stance to life of listening and accepting life as it is.

When I was four years old I moved to Amsterdam; a bit further along the canal from where we lived there was a beautiful Catholic church, called *The Little Dove*. Whenever I could, I would go in and just sit there, just saying a line from the Lord's Prayer my maternal grandfather had taught me, and soon I would be surrounded by blissful silence and enfolded in love. Wherever I was from then on, whatever happened in my outer life, this became part of my way of being; that inner silence and that love was my refuge and my point of balance.

Consequently, my image of God has always been of a God of Love, a guiding and supporting Divine Reality: a sense of being held, protected, supported, even when times were very hard. My faith is expressed in the saying from the *Desiderata:* "No doubt, the universe is unfolding as it should!" Because of my immediate experiences of this Reality at several stages in my life there has never been uncertainty in my mind as to the existence of a Higher Reality.

Soon after I arrived in England in my late teens I met my husband. He had different religions in his background: his father was Hindu and his mother was Christian. He, like me, had no particular attachment to the outward forms of religion, but had a deep spiritual faith.

An uncle of his, a respected judge, encouraged us to meditate with eastern techniques. I felt totally at ease with that, as it was very similar to what I had been doing all these years, sitting and repeating the Lord's Prayer until silence and love reigned. When my daughter was five years old and attending the local Church of England School, she asked us one day why we did not go to *her* church. So we joined that church. I felt I had reconnected with my roots and the faith of my beloved grandparents; but I carried on with meditation, as life without it seemed unimaginable.

Whereas at first my experience of meditation infused my life mainly on an unconscious level, moulding my being, I became with time more consciously aware of the transformative aspects of meditation. It deepened my awareness of that other Reality, influenced my attitude to life and other people and changed my reactions to the situations in which I found myself. My study of psychology and later my training as a Spiritual Director both helped me to make sense of what was happening.

Then came one of those moments when Destiny plays her hand: a friend introduced me to the writings of Bede Griffiths; I learned to my great joy that there was also a tradition of mantra meditation within Christianity. Soon after that another friend pointed me to a house, just down the road from where I live, where there was a community of the World Community for Christian Meditation meeting every week for meditation. So at last my Christian faith and my discipline of meditation came together and I had arrived *home*.

For many years now I have been teaching Christian meditation; the last seven years I have been leading the International School of the World Community for Christian Meditation. The more I share meditation with others worldwide the more I realise how revolutionary it is and how unprepared people are for the transformative effects it can have on their lives: hence this book. May it help you on your journey to the Source.

The journey into the inner self is not just the important one, it is the only one. We need to listen to the sound beyond the silence. (W.B.Yeats)

CHAPTER ONE

Meditation – the art of arts

Meditation is a powerful discipline for integration and transformation. By turning inwards in silence and solitude we re-tune the whole of our fragmented being and moreover become aware of our link to Ultimate Reality.

It works on three important integrally related levels: body, mind and spirit. The body/mind connection is clearly shown in the workings of the brain. The changes that are brought about in this way often require a real shift of perspective, which may well feel like a leap into the unknown. Courage and perseverance are needed, as the ego tries to resist the changes involved. The self, however, helps us through intuitive insights.

Achievement is a term of the ego and has no place here. The real end result is a spiritual gift. Not psychic side-effects but compassion is a sign that real growth has taken place.

* * * * *

We are a beautifully interconnected energetic system that is integrally linked into a wider cosmic whole. Yet we live as if we end at our skin boundary, independent and separate from others and from the environment. Even within this outer membrane we see ourselves as made up of separate parts: body, mind and spirit. Not only that, but we also have a strong tendency to put value on only one part and deny another one any importance at all – perhaps the body rather than the mind, or the mind rather than the body, the material *ego* rather than the spiritual *self*, one aspect of the *ego* rather than another. The result is fragmentation and lack of balance. We need to become aware of what we are doing, start accepting that all these aspects are of equal value and form an unbroken whole. At one level we do know that body, mind and spirit are different aspects of our total being and are therefore closely connected and affect one another: our body reflects the state of our mind and our connectedness with our spirit. When we communicate with one another, we do this on all three levels. Yet on another level we totally ignore this. The problem is especially acute with regard to the *ego/self*.

We have been given a physical body that allows us to operate in this material plane. Moreover, by means of our senses it allows us to interact with the environment in which we find ourselves. We have emotions and desires to deepen our experiences and we have a mind able to plan, rationalise and analyse. Those are the means that allow us to experience, learn and survive in this world. The problem is that we forget that they are the means and not the end. They constitute only one part of our created being, our *ego*, which is impermanent and subject to constant change.

We also have a deeper, unchanging and eternal element, the *self*, that is our link with the eternal nature of Divine Reality. Many philosophers, theologians and even some scientists like David Bohm believe that we and all creation are *enfolded* in the beginning in essence in the Ultimate Reality in the form of "seminal ideas." (St Augustine) The moment of creation is an *unfolding*, a projecting out of these eternal ideas. Our essence therefore remains in actual fact part of the Divine. Through the centuries this *essence* of humanity has been given many names: the *nous*, *the spark of reason, the spark of the soul, the spark of love, the Christ consciousness* and the *true self.*

The *ego* through its preoccupation with survival causes us to forget who we really are. The *self* calls us and tries to remind us that we are more than meets the eye. The spiritual path is a way of integrating these two aspects of our being, of remembering and reconnecting with the *eternal* inside us and outside us.

The body/mind connection

The effects of meditation clearly show the connection between the parts we tend to separate from each other. Changes on the level of the *body* result in alterations to our *mental* attitude to the situation in which we find ourselves and allow us to access the *spirit*.

Research has proved that meditation produces important

physiological effects on the body – lowering of breathing rate, blood pressure and heart rate – due to the relaxation response. This counteracts the effects of stress, anxiety and even pain. In doing so, moreover, it decreases the urge involved in addictions of many kinds, which are a negative way of trying to lower stress. Patients suffering from serious illnesses, such as heart disease and cancer, find that this decrease in tension improves their general health, mental outlook, and even seems to halt or slow down the progress of the disease.

The healing relaxation response is a result of distinct changes in the brain triggered by meditation. The pre-frontal cortex in our brain is involved with thoughts, images and daydreams, as well as attention. By focusing our mind in one-pointed attention, for instance on a mantra, we encourage increased activity in these attention cells. As our focus deepens, the activity in the cells involved in thoughts and images decreases considerably; this is reflected in a lessening of beta waves, our thinking waves – the *ego* part of our consciousness. Prolonged one-pointed attention also activates cells in the temporal lobe and increased activity there triggers changes in the limbic system, the region dealing with emotional response. The emotion of fear expressed in the strong survival *flight or fight* response changes to one of acceptance, relaxation and tranquillity – the relaxation response. These changes are reflected in the increase in *alpha* and *theta* waves.

Paying attention to our mantra therefore has led to the brain switching to different brain cells, which has resulted in a general feeling of relaxation and a lessening of thoughts. However, this is only the beginning. As meditation becomes even deeper, so does the relaxation response.[1]

This deepening in turn has a knock-on effect ending in a decreased activity in the parietal cortex, an area in the brain associated with orientation in time and space and creating boundaries: self/non-self, and the world of opposites – in fact, very much the qualities of the *ego*. This decrease in activity is in turn reflected in a lessening of these abilities, explaining why there is a sense of our separate identity – and time and space – dissolving and all opposites unifying. This leads to a feeling of connectedness with what surrounds us: in fact a sign of the deeper *self* coming to the fore.

The importance of this sequence is that the initiative for these changes stems from consciousness and the will: we are deliberately kick-starting the brain into a different mode of perception by one pointed focus. It is interesting to see how our *ego* consciousness, with its survival needs in this material plane, is encoded in the circuitry of the brain, but can be temporarily by-passed. In doing so we "cleanse the doors of perception and see reality as it is, infinite!" (William Blake) We return to our *original* nature, which is interwoven with the rest of creation and the cosmic All.

---

[1] In this respect I highly recommend for you to read: *Using Your Brain* by Dr Shanida Nataraja (to be published 2006)

It is perfectly possible to use meditation purely for its health benefits as a body and mind altering relaxation technique and stop there. It is wonderful to stop the endlessly chattering mind and release stress and tension. It will feel great to have time out from the concerns, anxieties, hopes and fears that generally beset us, to stop the drain of energy of a mind going round and round in circles. But that would be a missed opportunity; there is much more to meditation than its physiological effects on the body. The effects on the body and the mind are nevertheless an important first step on the road to transformation, to clarity of vision and total awareness.

The mind

For a serious practioner, relaxing the body is seen as an essential preparation, leading to the real purpose of meditation of totally transforming the mind. To do that, meditation needs to be a spiritual discipline involving solitude and silence in which we let go of all sense experiences, images, emotions and thoughts.

The resulting clarity of vision will also help us become aware of emotions and desires that have a tendency to overwhelm us and influence our behaviour. It will affect the *ego* in all its aspects and result in its transformation and transparency that allows us access to our essence, our *self*. It pierces the veils, which hide true knowledge of ourselves, the reality we live in and Ultimate Reality, granting a direct and unmediated experience of the Divine.

Once we have broken through, once we have crossed into

infinite reality we do not make our world there. That would be as unbalanced as accepting only the material world. The material reality is energetically denser than the higher reality. We have to allow the light to shine from this higher reality into our ordinary reality, so that our vision becomes enlightened, clarified and balanced.

This will inevitably effect a transformation of consciousness and thus a transformation of the whole person. It will fundamentally change us from people living at the surface to fully alive human beings. It allows us to realise our full potential, which all main religions and wisdom traditions encourage: "I have come that they may have life, life in all its fullness." (Gospel of John)

How much knowledge of another level changes the view of the reality we live in really depends on the individual and his/her destiny. For some of us living on the surface, doing what we feel is right, is fulfilling enough. Just the acceptance of the existence of different levels is often enough to enrich and inform our lives. Others find living only on the surface pointless. The lack of real meaning leads to a sense of absurdity, as exemplified in Joseph Heller's *Catch 22*. The pilots in this WW II story, who flew more missions than was really advisable, were quite unhinged, which meant they really should be grounded. But they only could be grounded if they asked for it. But if they asked for it, they were sane and therefore could not be grounded!

When we interpret life only at the surface level with its own weird logic it can begin to seem unreal, meaningless and even absurd. We feel that we are then merely "a poor player that struts and frets his hour upon the stage" living in a world of pure illusion. (Shakespeare, *Macbeth*)

Thoughts

To be able to alter our mind we need first to become aware of its habitual nature; only insight and awareness lead to change. Without these we will continue to operate only from the *ego* aspect of our consciousness and we will only get glimpses of our deeper *self*: the two will only superficially interact, if at all. By learning to watch the mind we are helping the process of integration of these two elements.

Only after relaxing the body, however, do we become fully aware of our mind whirring with thoughts. Ramakrishna compared the mind to a tree full of monkeys chattering, and jumping from branch to branch. This is a common characteristic of our mind and it goes on all the time, even when we are not aware of it. The more the distractions of our body decrease the more our awareness of our thoughts increases. We realise what a jumble our mind is. We soon appreciate that these thoughts form a powerful barrier on the path of meditation. When we observe them, we distinguish that some are trivial, inconsequential things we heard or saw in the media and entertainment, which prevent us from achieving stillness and harmony.

But there are also deeper thoughts that often revolve round more important issues we consider essential to survival in the world we live in, such as our self-image, our job and our relationships.

We soon become conscious of how influential our thoughts are in terms of the way we see reality, how we feel about ourselves, others and the world we live in. They all depend on the conditioned background of our thoughts, which indeed define our view: "The limits of my language (i.e. thoughts) are the limits of my world." (Wittgenstein)

My world is entirely different from yours, although we may live in similar circumstances in the same country. We do not see people and situations as they really are, but coloured by our thoughts, opinions, prejudices, experience and emotions.

Moreover, most of our thoughts whirl around our own concerns in some way or the other, in the form of memories, both good and bad, fears, hopes, desires and plans. In fact, we could easily say that we walk around in a landscape of our own mind, a world of illusion of our own making. What is illusion and what is reality?

"We are such stuff as dreams are made on; and our little life is rounded with a sleep." (Shakespeare, *The Tempest*)

This creation of our mind can be so powerful that it may seem the only reality that exists. It can mask the existence of a Higher Reality.

The two important elements here are firstly that this reality built up out of our thoughts and feelings is confined to the surface part of our being, the *ego*, and is shaped by illusions of the past and future. The *self* is not affected at all, as it exists purely in the present moment. There we are "children of God" and "temples of the Holy Spirit." (St Paul) Secondly, this surface reality we create is impermanent, subject to constant change linked to our attitude: "it alters when it alteration finds." (Shakespeare, *Sonnets*)

Change

Moreover this also applies to the field of operation of the *ego*: the actual material world. The inevitability of change in the world and in our life within it has been expressed since the dawn of time. Everything flows, nothing stays the same: "we cannot step in the same river twice." (Heraclites 5th century, BCE) If change is the only constant, then the positive aspect of this is that our awareness of the external reality we find ourselves in *can* change significantly.

We are often trapped in the thought, however, that change is *not* possible and especially when we have convinced ourselves that our attitude or opinion is right. Change of any kind can be seen as threatening to our security and survival. It is fear of change, fear of the unknown that holds us back. The *ego*, the King of Survival, uses this fear to prevent change. Consequently we prefer the known suffering of trying to swim upstream against the flow of change. We have to go beyond this fear, and realise that its nature too is illusory. We need courage and perseverance to face the fear that causes our blindness. We have to accept that there is no permanence on this earth, only challenge and growth. Only thus can we truly see, face outmoded ways of thinking and behaving, and embrace the creative opportunity for growth change represents. Only then does our hidden potential become visible.

To do this, meditation is helpful by brushing aside the veils made by the *ego* that hide our deeper *self*. Then we are susceptible to the loving promptings coming from the *self*, which help us to become aware of what motivates the *ego*. Then *fear* is replaced by an awareness of *love*.

By bringing unconscious drives to consciousness, by acknowledging and accepting them, deep change happens, often unnoticed. It does not happen overnight, but is a slow gradual process that imperceptibly alters us.

In all this we are not trying to suppress the *ego* – and live solely from the *self*. That would create just as dangerous an imbalance as purely living from the *ego* would. What we are striving for is temporarily silencing the surface mind, so we can become aware in the resulting interior stillness and silence of this deeper aspect of our consciousness. The superficial glimpses we had of the real *self* by grace become then an enduring and meaningful awareness.

Self-consciousness versus self-knowledge

The importance awarded to insight resulting in self-knowledge is brought out by the essential advice given by spiritual teachers and philosophers throughout history: *Man know thyself.*

We are encouraged to get to know the ego and the way it is motivated, which will lead not only to the possibility of change but also true self-knowledge: an awareness of our total being and of the Divine within. "When you know yourselves, then you will be known, and you will understand that you are children of the living father. But if you do not know yourselves, then you dwell in poverty, and you are poverty." (Gospel of Thomas 3)

Whereas self-knowledge is essential, self-consciousness, however, forms a powerful barrier to knowledge of our deeper *self* and blinds us to the trans-personal reality. Self-consciousness is of course *the* unique feature of humans which distinguishes us as far as we know from other sentient beings. But the problem is that we use this ability in a restricted way; instead of it being a consciousness of the whole *Self*, we limit and focus it narrowly on all the surface thoughts of the *ego*. We use self-consciousness then exclusively as a survival tool. Most of our thoughts then whirl around our own concerns in some way or another, trying to learn from our past and plan for the future for the sake of survival. Our memories of the past can of course be a constructive help in shaping the present and planning for the future. But we can also be caught in the snare of painful conditioned memories and consequent fears and anxieties for an uncertain future.

It is not that our *ego* is not important. Especially in the first part of our life we depend on our *ego* and we need it to be healthy and well-adapted. This is the first part of a development Jung called the *individuation* process. Moreover, we will always retain the need for the wisdom of the *ego*, as our survival skills will continue to be necessary for dealing maturely and realistically with both the external and internal world. We need to remember that the *ego* consciousness we are rightly proud of is on the surface and ever-changing, determined by our current pre-occupations. It is the deeper permanent wisdom of the *self* residing in the Unconscious that we need to bring to consciousness. We need an *ego* development that goes hand in hand with the growing awareness of the spiritual *self*: "One who knows all but is lacking in oneself is utterly lacking" (Gospel of Thomas 67). We need a shift in emphasis from the *ego* to the *self*. We need an *ego* that sees the wider picture, a conscious centre that accepts unconscious material into its vision and that sees itself as an integral part of the whole. This is the second part of the individuation process where we come to a "synthesis of the conscious and unconscious elements in the personality." Jung asserted that the achievement of this psychological integration and wholeness was all important. Then we operate from a balanced base using all of our resources, all our abilities conscious and unconscious, rational and intuitive. All will then infuse and inform our life, allowing us to tap into Cosmic Love and Wisdom. We need in fact a conscious return to our *original* consciousness before the *ego* circuit was put into place.

This true self-knowledge is not for its own sake, but as a stepping stone to experiencing the Ultimate Reality: "the reality we call God has first to be discovered in the human heart; moreover I cannot come to know God unless I know myself." (Meister Eckhart).

Escape strategies

If we misunderstand meditation and merely see it as a form of relaxation, a way of forgetting our problems, of escaping into our imagination and fantasies, we can practice for years without any increase in awareness or a resulting transformation. In fact it will merely reinforce the illusions we have of ourselves and others. Rather than coming to self-knowledge, we use meditation to suppress parts of our nature we do not like to be confronted with and we remain fragmented. We need to be open to insight furnished by our deeper *self* and show a willingness to acknowledge and accept ourselves as we actually are.

Moreover, rather than concentrating on truly understanding ourselves, we prefer to avoid change by focusing on trying to understand rationally and intellectually the Higher Reality we feel drawn to. The one thing philosophy and theology soon teach us is the basic impossibility of our limited rational capabilities to achieve such an understanding. There are no ultimate right answers; ideas often contradict and supplant previous attempts. All theories and theologies are limited personal attempts at interpretation.

"It is impossible to meditate on time and the mystery of the creative passage of nature without an overwhelming emotion at the limitations of human intelligence." (Alfred Whitehead)

Thomas Aquinas is a case in point. After a lifetime of writing and theorising about the Divine, he had a spiritual *experience,* which made him intensely aware of the uselessness of our attempts at rationalising. He saw all his writing as *straw* and wrote no more. He stressed the importance of the experience.

The quest for understanding is a natural and laudable one. But it is our *ego* aspect that loves to theorise about Ultimate Reality and is always fascinated by other people's attempts, even to the extent of wanting to surpass them. Hence the result is not wisdom, but knowledge leading to serious conflicts. The interpretation of the spiritual experience of our enlightened teachers, such as Jesus and the Buddha, of what they and their teaching meant, caused argument and division soon after their death.

But theorising, philosophising, theologising is a pleasant safe activity. It is an ideal way of avoiding the real work that needs to be done. It is no good speculating on the Divine and trying to become one with the Divine, if we do not spend our energy on identifying the things that hinder us from intuitively *experiencing* this Ultimate Reality.

The spirit

Whereas there is work for us to do on our mind and body, spiritual transformation itself is outside our control. This total change of consciousness cannot be achieved in any way, but is a gift of divine grace.

Although the spiritual journey is here presented in a linear fashion, first body, then mind, then spirit, these levels are not progressive stages but simultaneous, overlapping, deepening levels. We spiral through them, being afforded glimpses, as we practise.

Often at the start of the spiritual journey there is already a sudden deep spiritual insight, a remembering of our true nature, a glimpse of a wider dimension and a turning away from preoccupation with the surface reality. We remember that the *Light* already dwells within us; we are already *enlightened*: "We have come from the light, from the place where the light came into being by itself, established itself..... We are its children". (Gospel of Thomas 50) The early church Fathers called this the moment of conversion or *metanoia*; a change of heart and mind, an insightful conversion that allows the memory of our true *self* to become clearer over time. This will enable us to step over the threshold between the different levels of perception. It literally means a change in the *nous*. *Nous* is the word Plato used to delineate our human *essence*, but it also included our mind. When we enter our inner being on the contemplative path, we leave our rational intelligence, our emotions and our sense perceptions behind and operate purely from the faculty superior to reason in the *nous*: our intuitive intelligence. This is our link and channel of communication with the Divine. We now call it our deeper *self*, our spiritual nature. The *self* is unaffected by the outer events of our life and is free to help us with its insights and intuitions.

These are granted after the silence of meditation or in dreams and in other ways our spiritual self has found to reach us.

The impetus for *metanoia* is often a crisis point or major life event at any stage in our lives, when the seemingly secure and unchanging reality we live in is bewilderingly turned upside down. We are rejected by an individual or a group; we face failure, loss of esteem; we lose a treasured job or our health suddenly fails us. The result can be either a refusal to accept the change, a descent into negativity, mistrust and despair. Or faced with the fact that our reality is not as immutable as we considered it to be, we may rise to the challenge to look at ourselves, our habitual framework, our opinions and values with different eyes.

It is in such a moment, when the chain made up out of all our conditioning, all our thoughts, memories and emotions momentarily breaks, that we stand free and unhindered in the "here and now" – the eternal moment. For an instant we see reality as it is. What this really means is clearly demonstrated by Mary Magdalene. After Jesus' crucifixion she goes to the tomb to find it empty. She is distraught, wrapped up in her own pain and anguish. Even when Jesus appears she is so overwhelmed by her grief that she cannot see clearly. She does not recognise him and takes him for the gardener. The moment Jesus calls her by name she breaks through her clouded vision of reality with its focus on her own emotions and needs and sees him in his true reality.

Eckhart Tolle in his book *The Power of Now* describes the crisis that started him on his journey. From a perpetual feeling of dread, the world alien, hostile and meaningless, including his own life, he arrived instantaneously at the realisation of the true nature of himself and Reality. Out of the moment of deepest despair sprung up the essential question, "Who am I really?" and through the void, by truly letting go of everything, he was reborn into the awareness of the Ultimate Reality which gives light and life to our ordinary reality.

Bede Griffiths' awareness of true Reality did not spring out of a crisis but out of contemplation of Nature. He describes in *The Golden String* how he was led by the beauty of bird song and hawthorn bushes in full bloom to a profound feeling of awe at the sight of the setting sun, whilst a lark "poured out its song." He felt that he "was made aware of another world of beauty and mystery" and, especially at evening, he felt on many other occasions too the "presence of an unfathomable mystery."

Some people will consciously recognise the similarity between their own state of mind at the start of their search in one or the other of the experiences described above; with others it resonates at an unconscious level.

Not always is this moment as dramatic. Our perceptual awareness varies enormously from person to person, from moment to moment. Some of us may have had a moment of *transcendence*, an awareness of a different reality, an escape from the prison of the *ego*, whilst listening to music, poetry or being absorbed in a work of art. Others may never have been consciously aware of an actual moment of insight, and yet at some level may always have been aware of the existence of a higher reality. They are without knowing becoming gradually more in tune with this reality. Quite early on in meditation we often touch the experience of real peace and even joy bubbling up. Moments like these when we are released from self-preoccupation are Divine gifts.

In any case this glimpse is not the end, but the beginning – an impetus for growth. The longing to know more about this intuited reality gets stronger and we look round for those who could help us to approach it. At this point we often discover meditation in one form or another. It is the start of the work of clarifying and integrating the experience and so allowing the ascent to spiritual awareness, personal authenticity and a transpersonal truth.

This sudden timeless insight, however fleeting and impermanent, may well have lasting effects, but work, effort and grace are needed to effect a permanent transformation. A dance is needed, a dance of integration of the *ego* and its *shadow*, of the *ego* and the *self*, of the *self* and the Ultimate Reality.

The Perennial Philosophy

The possibility of integration of the *self* with Ultimate Reality is clearly expressed in the *Perennial Philosophy*[2], which describes the common ground of all the world's great religions and philosophies. It is important to remember that the commonality

---

[2] For clarification and justification of the idea of a *Perennial Philosophy* the best books are Aldous Huxley, *The Perennial Philosophy* and Matthew Fox, *One River, Many Wells*.

this philosophy stresses is founded in actual practical spiritual experience that takes place outside the time and space of our usual material reality. Moreover, Bede Griffiths says: "When the human mind reaches a certain point of experience it comes to this same understanding and this is what constitutes the *Perennial Philosophy*." He refers to the intuitive way of understanding and not the rational one, a predominately right-brain function rather than a left-brain one.

The *Perennial Philosophy* confidently states that there is an Ultimate Reality that is both universally immanent in creation and transcendent to it. The reality we can apprehend with the senses is embedded in and sustained by this all pervading Reality. The essential quality of this Higher Reality is that it cannot be reached by the senses and the rational mind: it cannot be expressed clearly by thoughts or images; it is incomprehensible and ineffable. Yet there is something in the deeper eternal *self* of a human being, beyond the personal *ego*, which has something in common with this Ultimate Reality and can therefore truly relate to it. It is the ground of our individual being that we share with others and with the whole of creation; it is there that we are all one.

We all possess this *essence* – the *self*. The *Perennial Philosophy* holds out the firm conviction that everyone, not just special 'mystical' types, can therefore reach union with Ultimate Formlessness, irrespective of how this is expressed: *nirvana, no-mind, enlightenment, Union with the Godhead.* By practicing meditation as a serious contemplative spiritual discipline we become personally aware of this innate potential for all-embracing unity and are gradually transformed by grace to be more and more in tune with this higher level of consciousness.

The energy of the *self* aspect of our being will resonate with the similar energy in the Divine Reality:

All that is limited by form, semblance, sound and colour,
is called object.
Among them all, man alone
is more than an object.
Though, like objects, he has form and semblance,
He is not limited to form. He is more.
He can attain to formlessness.
(Chang Tzu)

Spiritual achievements

There is nothing to strive for; it is not an *achievement*. We just need to remember this Divine gift is inherent in our human nature. The hope and trust coming from the knowledge of this innate potential does make our practice meaningful and lifts it from the realm of mere relaxation. All traditions stress that there is no ultimate *achievement* and any of the so-called *achievements* along the spiritual path are only by-products and should not be given any attention.

Achievement, goal are words of the *ego* and therefore not relevant on this path. However, again this is going against the grain, as we are strongly conditioned to value achievements and are programmed to give them high priority.

21

The Desert Fathers and Mothers of the 4th century (see Epilogue) also saw the quest for *achievement* as caused by misdirected emotional *ego* forces: demons. The Buddha too thought little of achievements, calling them the vehicle of the *ego*:

The Buddha was walking along the bank of a river and came across a saddhu, who was sitting in apparent deep meditation. When the man came out of it, the Buddha asked him what he was doing so intently. "I want to cross the river by walking over the water."

"I see," the Buddha said and walked on.

Over the next twenty years the Buddha came across this man on several occasions, still trying but not yet having reached his goal. Finally one day as the Buddha was passing by, the Saddhu with a great smile of achievement on his face, shouted to the Buddha that he at last could walk on water. The Buddha complimented him, but then gently inquired whether it would not have been simpler just to pay the ferry man.

Sudden insights, shifts of awareness, the *kensho* experience, and *enlightenment* cannot be brought about by sheer effort. The more we try to achieve them, the further they seem to recede.

Transformation will occur only when we *let go* of our striving to achieve and of willed effort of any kind that traps us in our surface mind. Then *grace* can enter in. The desired attitude is one of detachment from all that might or might not happen, beautifully illustrated in this saying from *The Way of Chuang Tzu:*

When an archer is shooting for nothing
He has all his skill.
If he shoots for a brass buckle
He is already nervous.

If he shoots for a prize of gold
He goes blind.
Or sees two targets-
He is out of his mind!

His skill has not changed. But the prize
Divides him. He cares.
He thinks more of winning
Than of shooting
And the need to win drains him of power.

Spiritual versus psychic

The importance of spiritual, moral and emotional development occurring side by side cannot be stressed enough. The higher awareness obtained in meditation, the next stage in our spiritual evolutionary growth, must lead to an actual change of the entire being, thereby leading to balance and harmony. Without all these aspects growing side by side a potentially dangerous one-sidedness can arise. It is not unusual to see teachers who are spiritually and psychically advanced, whose moral, emotional development and interpersonal skills are sorely lacking, with far from desirable consequences.

The energy released in following a contemplative practice

can be used for insight and transformation on all levels leading to the spiritual plane. Alternatively, the *ego* not willing to let go of its dominant position can feed on this, prevent further growth and hijack the so-called *achievements* on the spiritual path. Jung called this the danger of *inflation.* Contact with the deeper *self,* the Spirit, then results in an exaggerated view of oneself. We think we are special; we feel superior, boastfully looking down on others; we know better, we know it all. And before we know it, we suffer from a superiority complex, which over time can become megalomania. The *ego* has appropriated all that the spiritual depth of our nature has made possible. It may lead to posturing and overdoing the practice. Since it is done in the wrong frame of mind this is counterproductive and can even be potentially dangerous.

One of these *achievements* is the re-emergence of psychic abilities, which the *ego* confuses with the purpose of the journey. Psychic abilities may well have been basic human powers we all possessed in former times. They may have been important at an early stage in our evolutionary development before we had acquired the ability of using complex language. With the development of language these earlier abilities could then have been neglected.

But the new evolutionary stage of our development may well require the building of links between the older and the newer intellectual and intuitive abilities: hence the re-emergence of psychic abilities when we meditate. In neuro-physiological terms neural pathways are being activated between the left side of the brain – the rational aspect – and the right side of the brain – the intuitive, holistic aspect. The brain is following the lead initiated by our discipline, integrating in the same way that we are.

However, concentrating on and over-emphasizing these abilities are retrograde steps. Real spiritual growth is hindered and stagnation is the result. We stay very much on the material plane; in fact the *ego* traps us in that reality. Occasional glimpses of a spiritual dimension may be experienced, but the true meaning of this will not be understood. It is seen as another *achievement*, reaching another level of human potential, a sign of having reached a higher level of consciousness; again it is used to feed the *ego*. The result is that no transformation or integration of the whole of our being, no emerging of the *self* based on these experiences can take place. The physical benefits of meditation and awareness of different levels of consciousness would be apparent, but emotional baggage and conditioning will continue to distort the perspective on reality and adversely influence our actions in life. Self-interest rather than compassion will be the driving force in the individual.

Guidance

The tradition warns that the further we move along the spiritual path the more dangerous these temptations of *achievements* motivated by vainglory and pride become.

Therefore going it alone is considered by all traditions to be very dangerous, leading easily not only to self-delusion and pride but even madness: "Some old men said, 'If you see a young man climbing up to the heavens by his own will, catch him by the foot and throw him down to the earth; it is not good for him.'" (Writings of the Desert Fathers)

Although over time the silence and stillness of meditation leads us to find the inner Teacher, the Christ within, who furnishes insights into the ground of our behaviour, it is still recommended to have these insights or experiences checked by a teacher or a more experienced fellow traveller. To discern whether these insights come from the *ego* or are divinely inspired and reach us through the *self* requires experience based on practice. This is one of the reasons for the emphasis in Christian meditation on attending a regular meditation group. Moreover, meditation is seen in the framework of a spiritual life with faith and trust in the benevolent nature of the Ultimate Reality as key elements. It is considered to be a complementary aspect that deepens and completes the whole of the spiritual discipline of prayer. "Meditation is the missing dimension of much Christian life today. It does not exclude other types of prayer and indeed deepens reverence for the sacraments and scripture." (Laurence Freeman)

There is a salutary tale about going it alone in the writing of the Desert Fathers:

Remember the old man Hero who was cast down from the heights to the lowest depths because of a diabolical illusion. I remember how he remained fifty years in the desert, keeping to the rigours of abstinence with a severity that was outstanding, loving the secrecy of the solitary life with fervour marvellously greater than that of anyone else dwelling here. After such toil how and why could he have been fooled by the deceiver? How could he have gone down into so great a ruin that all of us here in the desert were stricken with pain and grief? Surely the reason for it was that he had too little of the virtue of discernment and that he preferred to be guided by his own ideas rather than to bow down to the advice and conferences of his brethren and to the rules laid down by our predecessors. He practised fasting so rigorously and so relentlessly, he was so given to the loneliness and secrecy of his cell, that even the special respect due to Easter day could not persuade him to join the brethren in their meal. He was the only one who could not come together with all his brethren and assembled in church for the feast, and the reason for this was that by taking the tiniest share of the vegetables he might give the impression of having relaxed from what he had chosen to do.

This presumptuousness led to his being fooled. He showed the utmost veneration for the angel of Satan, welcoming him as if he were actually an angel of light. Yielding totally to his bondage he threw himself headlong into a well, whose depths no eye could penetrate. He did so trusting completely in the assurance of the angel who had guaranteed that on account of the merit of his virtues and of his works he could never come to any harm. To experience his undoubted freedom from danger the deluded man threw himself in darkness of night into his well. He would know first-hand the great

merit of his own virtue when he emerged unscathed. His brothers,
who had to struggle very hard at it, pulled him out half dead. He
would die two days later. Worse, he was to cling firmly to his illusion,
and the very experience of dying could not persuade him that he
had been the sport of devilish skill. Those who pitied him his leaving
had the greatest difficulty in obtaining the agreement of Abba
Paphnutius that for the sake of the merit won by his very hard work
and by the many years endured by him in the desert he should not
be classed among the suicides, and hence, be deemed unworthy of
remembrance and prayers offered for the dead." (John Cassian –
Conferences 2, 5)

Not only does the Desert tradition stress the value of
guidance, but at the same time it warns us to be careful in the
choosing of our guides: "a teacher ought to be a stranger to the
desire for domination, vain-glory, and pride; one should not be
able to fool him by flattery, nor blind him by gifts, nor conquer
him by the stomach, nor dominate him by anger; but he should
be patient, gentle and humble as far as possible; he must be tested
and without partisanship, full of concern, and a lover of souls."
(Amma Theodora)

Teaching must be based on personal experience, not just
theoretical knowledge. "It is dangerous for anyone to teach who
has not first been trained in the practical life. For if someone
who owns a ruined house receives guests there, harm is done
because of the dilapidation of the dwelling. It is the same in the
case of someone who has not first built an interior dwelling; loss

is caused to those who come. By words one may convert them to salvation, but by evil behaviour, one injures them." (Amma Syncletica)

Compassion

If we are not tempted by *achievements*, meditation will lead to transformation. The outward sign that this has taken place and Ultimate Reality has become manifest in an individual is growth in compassion, a selfless loving without attachments to results or expectations guided by true wisdom.

Compassion and enlightenment, realising the Ultimate Reality, are inexorably linked, but compassion has priority. "It can happen that when we are at prayer some brothers come to see us. Then we have to choose, either to interrupt our prayer or to sadden our brother by refusing to answer him. But love is greater than prayer. Prayer is one virtue amongst others, whereas love contains them all." (John Climacus 7th century)

We have all experienced that it is difficult to be genuinely happy if we are at odds with people we care about. The spiritual path helps us to close the gap between ourselves, others and creation. If we experience the true reality of ourselves, we are aware that others too have the *Christ* within, or in Buddhist terms *Buddha nature*. It becomes easier to accept others and take their feelings and thoughts into account by walking round in their shoes.

The world will, as a result, become a more peaceful place;

not by our changing the world, but by changing our own attitude from one of self-interest to one of being concerned about one another, regardless of family connections, background, culture or religion. "Be the change you want to see in the world." (Gandhi) This too was the essence of Jesus' teaching.

The following story brilliantly illustrates the transformation needed on the spiritual path:

Awid Afifi, the Tunisian, was a 19th-century dervish teacher who drew his wisdom from the wide expanse of desert North Africa. He once shared with his pupils a story that began with a gentle rain falling on a high mountain in a distant land. The rain was at first hushed and quiet, trickling down granite slopes. Gradually it increased in strength, as rivulets of water rolled over the rocks and down the gnarled, twisted trees that grew there. The rain fell as water must without calculation. The Sufi master understood that water never has time to practise falling. Soon it was pouring, as swift currents of dark water flowed together into the beginnings of a stream. The brook made its way down the mountainside through small standards of cypress trees and fields of lavender tipped purslane, down cascading falls. It moved without effort, splashing around stones – learning that a stream interrupted by the rocks is the one that sings most nobly. Finally, having left its heights in the distant mountain, the stream made its way to the edge of a great desert. Sand and rock stretched beyond seeing. Having crossed every other barrier in its way the stream fully expected to cross this as well. But as fast as its waves splashed into the desert, that fast did they disappear into the sand. Before long the wind heard a voice whispering, as if coming from the desert itself, saying, "The wind crosses the desert, so can the stream." "Yes, but the wind can fly!" cried out the stream, still dashing itself into the desert sand. "You'll never get across that way," the desert whispered. "You have to let the wind carry you." "But how?" shouted the stream. "You have to let the wind absorb you." The stream could not accept this, however, not wanting to lose its identity or abandoned its own individuality. After all, if it gave itself to the wind, could it ever be sure of becoming a stream again? The desert replied that the stream could continue its flowing, perhaps one day even producing a swamp there at the desert's edge. But it would never cross the desert so long as it remained a stream. "Why can't I remain the same stream that I am?" the water cried. And the desert answered, ever so wisely, "You never can remain what you are. Either you become a swamp or you give yourself to the wind". The stream was silent for a long time, listening to distant echoes of memory, knowing parts of itself having been held before in the arms of the wind. From that long forgotten place, it gradually recalled how water conquers only by yielding, by flowing around obstacles, by turning to steam when threatened by fire. From the depths of that silence, slowly the stream raised its vapours to the welcoming arms of the wind and was born upward, carried easily on great white clouds over the wide desert waste. Approaching distant mountains on the desert's far side, the stream then began once again to fall as a light rain. At first it was hushed and quiet, trickling down granite slopes. Gradually it increased in strength, as rivulets rolled *over the rocks and down the gnarled, twisted trees that grew there. The rain fell, as water must, without calculation. And soon it was pouring, as swift currents of dark water flowed together – yet again – into the headwaters of a new stream. Awad Affifi refused to say what the story meant, how it should be interpreted. He simply pointed the students to the desert nearby and urged them to find out for themselves.* [3]

---

[3] Sufi teaching story quoted in Belden C. Lane, *The Solace of Fierce Landscapes*

CHAPTER TWO
Stilling the body and the mind

Before any integration can take place, we need to conquer the restlessness of both our body and mind that the ego causes. We still the mind by stilling the body and the breath.

But most important is an attitude of acceptance of the nature of our mind and its thoughts; we need to let go of the fear of not thinking and embrace the silence of the inner desert.

These are the key elements: attention and detachment. Fighting or suppressing thoughts is counterproductive. All traditions recommend a tool to detach ourselves from our thoughts and reach the one pointed focus that will lead us into the creative silence that dwells in our centre.

* * * * *

In our Western culture we have been conditioned until recently to disregard our body totally. We treat it on the whole as no more than a useful vehicle for our mind; we tend to live in the mind. But it is essential that we become aware of our body and give it due attention. We saw how integrally connected the body and the mind are. In fact, the body mirrors the mind: when we are agitated in our mind it will be apparent in our body. The health of our body in turn affects the quality of our mind.

It can therefore be helpful to try and relax and harmonise the body before meditation. The result of a quiet body will be a quiet mind. Disciplines that stress balance and integration, such as Yoga, Tai Chi and Chi Kung, are excellent ways of doing this. Becoming aware of our body and breath helps to cultivate, moreover, an attitude of alertness and awareness – an integral part of meditation.[1]

A relaxed upright position, with our back as straight as is comfortable for us, is also recommended by many traditions. It doesn't really matter whether we sit on a chair or in the full lotus position, as long as it allows us to hold our back straight but relaxed for the full duration of the meditation. The straight back and the relaxed shoulders also make sure that the chest is wide open, allowing enough oxygen to circulate around our system, helping us not to fall asleep. Our feet or knees need to be firmly planted on the ground, so our position is one of rootedness: "Posture is an outward sign of your inner commitment to the discipline of meditation...Becoming rooted in ourselves, we become rooted in our own proper place in creation." (John Main)

Most traditions also recommend sitting "with your palms upright or facing down with thumb and forefinger joined." (John

---

[1] See Appendix II for simple preparatory exercises

Main). In the Eastern tradition to have the thumb and forefinger touching is part of the circulation of energy. But it is also an excellent way of keeping alert: when our attention has slipped, we will find that our fingers are no longer touching either.

Restlessness and stability

To sit still and stay in one place is actually the first hurdle in the discipline of meditation. We are so used to being perpetually on the move doing things, that sitting still, not doing anything in particular, can seem a daunting and unusual task. The truth of this becomes immediately apparent when we are just sitting by ourselves in a room for more than ten to fifteen minutes, whether at home or elsewhere.

Instead of using the time to pay attention to our thoughts and ourselves in a constructive way, our restlessness tempts us into distracting thoughts of a trivial nature. We daydream or escape into worrying or planning. Quite soon, though, we become bored, we get up, wondering what there is to do. Is there something to look at? Is there something to read? Is there something else to do? We are so used to reacting to stimuli coming from outside, that we feel quite lost without them.

Restlessness is in our genes; our ancestors were all members of migratory tribes. A baby is a beautiful example of this. Every parent or carer knows a fretful baby will settle down with movement: rocking the cradle, carrying and walking, or taking them for a walk in the pram or pushchair. In trying to sit still, to stay in one place, we are actually going against the grain. Allowing our body to be still, giving it the permission not to do anything, is the first step of counteracting this restless tendency. It is only by persevering that the urge to move and do things lessens and we become aware of the advantages of stillness and silence. The Desert Fathers and Mothers, on whose teaching Christian meditation is based, stressed the importance of staying in one place. "A brother in Scetis went to ask for a word from Abba Moses and the old man said to him, *'Go and sit in your cell and your cell will teach you everything.'*"

Although restlessness is a truly human problem, it is even more pronounced in the West. We are always on the go, always engaged in some project or other and more often than not multi-tasking. Especially those of us who live in big cities really seem to be a people constantly on the move: travelling to work, to entertainment, to friends. Our restlessness also extends to a need for variety and change with respect to our jobs, the restaurants and bars we frequent and even the friends we have.

Our Western culture is dominated by the *ego* and its *doing* and *achieving*. We are very much conditioned to do rather than to be: *Don't just sit there, do something!* Already as children we are constantly kept busy, especially by parents who take their role seriously, in active or artistic pursuits. Sitting, being, dreaming is not really encouraged. It is not unusual to hear a child say "I am bored!" when it is not *doing* something just then or can't think of what to *do* next. This restlessness also manifests itself in the 'spiritual butterfly' syndrome: moving from one teacher to the next, never staying for a long period of time.

This restlessness was frowned upon in the Desert tradition: "If you find yourself in a monastery do not go to another place, for that will harm you a great deal. Just as the bird who abandons the eggs she was sitting on prevents them from hatching, so the monk or the nun grows cold and their faith dies when they go from one place to another."(Amma Syncletica)

St Benedict was very influenced by the Desert tradition through the writings of Cassian[2]. Stability is also a prime virtue in his Rule. In the very first Chapter of his Rule, he expresses real hostility toward restless monks whom he called *gyrovagues,* who are always on the move and never settle to put down roots of stability. In other Western monastic traditions, however, this was not emphasized. Nor was this the case in the Christian Orthodox, Hindu and Buddhist tradition, where it was quite acceptable to move from teacher to teacher.

This restlessness can also be expressed by frequently changing our discipline. Whereas we may try different methods for a while – many disciplines have basically the same effect in focusing the attention and are equally useful in entering the silence of true meditation – we eventually have to settle and be faithful to one discipline, to dig deep and be truly rooted. Otherwise we stay on the surface and will be like the farmer in this story:

---

[2] See *Epilogue – Roots of Christian Meditation*

A farmer wanted to dig a well on his land. He chose a field where there had been a well in the past. He started digging hard in one spot, really worked at it for a while, but when after some time he did not hit water, he gave up and started in a different spot. Again he started with full enthusiasm, but soon he again felt it wasn't working. He started in another spot and so on, until he had a field full of holes but no well! Had he dug in one spot he would have reached the water level, the Source, and water would have flowed of its own accord.

But stability – the opposite of restlessness – is essential. We need especially internally to stand on firm ground, spiritually and psychologically rooted. We need to become "the still point of the turning world". (T.S.Eliot) This rootedness will last not only for the duration of our meditation sessions but will eventually become an attitude of mind. This will transform our life and allow us to live and act permanently from that deep centre at the core of our being.

The breath

The breath is the bridge between the body and the mind. When the body is at rest, the breath gets quieter and so does the mind. If we are stressed or agitated, our breath is shallow and fast. If we are relaxed, our breath is slow and deep. Therefore if we work to still not only our body but also our breath, we will still our mind further.

The following passage from the *Philokalia* goes even further, sounding much like *Pranayama* exercises from Yoga: "You know, brother, how we breathe: we breathe the air in and out. On this is based the life of the body and on this depends its warmth. So, sitting down in your cell, collect your mind, lead it into the path of the breath along which the air enters in, constrain it to enter the heart altogether with the inhaled air, and keep it there. Keep it there, but do not leave it silent and idle; instead give it the following prayer: *Lord, Jesus Christ, Son of God, have mercy on me.*"

But these breathing exercises are only useful as a preparation to meditation; they are best put aside when starting to meditate properly. Once the breath has quietened down and flows naturally we may find it helpful to link our breath and our mantra, as this can help to root the mantra in our being. But if this distracts, just let go of the breath *(see Appendix II)*. In the selected verses of the following poem the importance of posture and breath in meditation is beautifully described:

> *When you meditate, be like a mountain*
> *Immovably set in silence.*
> *Its thoughts are rooted in eternity.*
> *Do not do anything, just sit, be*
> *And you will reap the fruit flowing from your prayer.*
>
> *When you meditate, be like a flower*
> *Always directed towards the sun.*
> *Its stalk, like a spine, is always straight.*
> *Be open, ready to accept everything without fear*

And you will not lack light on your way.

When you meditate, be like an ocean
Always immovable in its depth.
Its waves come and go.
Be calm in your heart
And thoughts will go away by themselves.

When you meditate, remember your breath:
Thanks to it man has come alive.
It comes from God and it returns to God.
Unite the word of prayer with the stream of life and
    nothing will separate you from the Giver of life.

Every mountain teaches us the sense of eternity,
Every flower, when it fades, teaches us the sense of
    fleetingness.
The ocean teaches us, how to retain peace among
    adversities,
And love always teaches us Love.

(Fr Seraphion of Mount Athos,
adapted by Fr Jan Bereza OSB)

Stilling the mind

When we begin to meditate, we soon become aware of the fact that the discipline is simple but not easy. Yet it is important to stress at this point that meditation builds on our innate human abilities: to sense at an intuitive level and to focus the attention.

When we have countered our outer restlessness, it will now try to find a different outlet: if we can't move physically, we let

our thoughts do the walking. We wander about in daydreams, down memory lane, planning, hoping, worrying; internally we are still filled with perpetual noise and movement, the mad whirl of disconnected thoughts. The Desert Fathers knew this inner restlessness as the *demon of acedia* that led the monk first to a longing for food and company, then to blaming others for his present frame of mind and finally to missing his former way of life and being tempted to return to the world.

We too are tempted to give up when we are trying to quieten the mind in meditation and feel assailed by all these thoughts. Soon we too start to feel discouraged and think that perhaps we are not meant to be doing this. However, the message from those who have preceded us on this journey is: *persevere!* Just focus on the breath and the mantra and accept what happens with equanimity. It is worth it: inner silence creates the awareness and centredness we are missing in everyday life.

Not until we actually try to let go of all our thoughts and

images, however, do we become aware of how essential our mind considers them to be to our sense of identity. As long as we are thinking, we know who we are and we feel we have a modicum of control over what happens, however illusory that may be. We feel we are in charge and therefore secure.

Moreover, we soon realise that we are actually addicted to thoughts, since we have been brought up in a worldview in which thought is considered to be the highest activity we can engage in. Descartes in his statement "I think, therefore I am", actually linked existence with thought. *Not thinking* feels like a threat to our survival. T.S Eliot brings this out in his *Four Quartets*, in which people sitting in an underground train stuck in a tunnel feel they are faced with "the growing terror of nothing to think about." We have to let go of this link between thought and being.

It is not surprising that people are fearful when faced with a discipline like meditation that encourages *letting go* of thought and even images, in fact all the operations of the rational mind: thinking, memory and imagination.

Qualities of the inner and outer desert

Silence and solitude are prerequisites for meditation. The Desert *Abbas* and *Ammas* certainly had no difficulty finding silence and solitude in the desert. Silence, however, is difficult to find in the Western world, although solitude is possible, even in a busy city. "There are many who live in the mountains and behave as if they were in the town, and they are wasting their time. It is possible to be a solitary in one's mind while living in a crowd, and it is possible for one who is a solitary to live in the crowd of personal thoughts." (Amma Syncletica)

However, we cannot all move to the actual desert, but meditation is in fact a way of entering the desert – the inner desert. Anyone who has ever been in the real desert will know that it is a dangerous and merciless place for the unwary. It is an environment where we are not in charge. So as not to get lost and to secure our survival, we need a guide who can teach us. We need to be attentive to the subtle signs of the desert which might indicate future hazards: the behaviour of animals, the wind and the weather. Moreover, we need to be responsive to our own feelings and moods, as they may indicate tiredness or dehydration.[3] The same safeguards are needed for travel in the inner desert. Undivided attention is needed on the mantra, so as not to get lost in our thoughts, as well as awareness of our own inner resistances.

Attention is therefore required on both the inner and the outer journey. But we also need *detachment*. In the inner desert we need to accept the solitude and silence and detach not only from the discomfort and boredom of sitting in one position and in one place but also from the chaos of our restless mind with its thoughts, sounds and images. In the external desert too, we need *detachment* from the scarcity of food and water, the intense heat by day and bitter cold by night.

---

[3] This comparison is beautifully explored in Beldon C. Lane's book, *The Solace of Fierce Landscapes*

It is no good fighting against these factors, since in both cases our aim can only be reached through accepting our lack of control. We need to learn to live with insecurity. We need to learn to live without always needing to know 'why'. We need to stay in the desert accepting the higher wisdom of our internal and external guide. Moreover we soon find that in both cases it is not reason but intuition that can guide us.

These qualities of *attention* and *detachment* may seem to be opposite, but they are in fact complementary. We need to know when "to care and not to care" (T.S.Eliot); we need to know when to focus our attention on something, and when to ignore what is inevitable.

Furthermore, the desert has always been considered a striking symbol of Ultimate Reality in its awesomeness and grandeur, its immensity and unknowability. In the inner desert we contact this same reality within our centre, our *self*. In both environments we need to strip ourselves of all inessentials. What props up our self-image in the outer material reality is of no use in the inner one. We need to purify the *ego* of its need for control and other desires. We need to be like the Desert Fathers and Mothers who in their search for their own true self in Christ "had to reject completely the false, formal self, fabricated under social compulsion in the *world*." (Thomas Merton)

Silence

The importance of dealing with the problem of thoughts

and distractions whirring through our mind is emphasized in all traditions and is summed up by the first statement in the Yoga Sutras of Patanjali – a near contemporary of Jesus: "*Yoga citta vritti nirodha.*" (Yoga [union] is the stilling of the movement of the mind.) Inner silence is a sign the *ego* is stilled; without this we cannot reach the deeper part of our consciousness, the *self.*

The stilling of the mind allows us to become aware of the essential stillness at the centre of our being. If we can free our mind from all that assaults it, we discover the deep peace and inconceivable clarity that lives within us.

To withdraw into the silence we need to let go of both external noises and our sense perceptions in general. This inner silence we are trying to reach is not just an absence of noise, but a creative energy that allows us to become *pro-active* out of our own creative impulses rather than *reactive* to external stimuli.

There are ways we can help ourselves achieve inner stillness. Aiming for external silence can help us to reach inner peace. Silence, however, is an elusive quality for most of us in our present environment in the West; we are constantly surrounded by external noise. Moreover, we are bombarded by trivia through the media, TV, music, internet, computer games. "We have the most extraordinary possibilities for communication in print, radio and television, and we are fed daily with nonsense which would be offensive to the intelligence of children were they not suckled on it." (Erich Fromm, *Psychoanalysis and Religion*) Furthermore we have become so used to noise that its absence feels strange and unfamiliar, therefore even threatening.

Yet we need to find the courage to create pockets of external and internal silence in our day in addition to our periods of meditation, where we don't talk to others, in person or on the phone, where we don't listen to the radio, TV or music. Mini-meditations on our journey to work or during our working day are another useful way of increasing our ability to detach ourselves from external noise, apart from other obvious benefits.

If we are living in a busy city a preparatory exercise can be helpful. First we become aware of the noises outside the house, really listen to them, note the variety, name them and then accept their presence with equanimity. Then we focus on those inside the house, acknowledge them, accept them as inevitable and then take our attention off them. Complete absence of noise is virtually impossible in the world we live in, as is proved by an account of an English woman living in a cave in the Himalayas being driven to distraction by the noise of the goats around her cave.

An attitude of acceptance

The most important way of dealing either with our noisy world or our own chaotic mind is to accept them as they are. Acceptance is one of the most difficult lessons to learn, but actually the most important one. We are so used to criticising and judging ourselves as well as others, that we get irritated when we sit down to meditate and the thoughts just crowd in or noises disturb us. But the more we get irritated with ourselves, the more we try to suppress our thoughts, the more persistent they become. Instead of unifying our mind we are dividing ourselves: one part of our mind fights another.

An image comes to mind. I remember hearing years ago about an advertisement for meditation. On a poster there stood an Indian Guru, in typical attire and appearance on his surfboard, balanced perfectly, riding the waves. Underneath was the phrase: "You can't stop the waves, but you can learn to surf."

We cannot suppress or get rid of our thoughts; they will be there just like the waves. We need to accept them as an inevitable part of ourselves and just ride them skilfully.

In Christian meditation our surfboard is the mantra. At times the thoughts and the waves calm down, the sea is smooth and calm – we lie peacefully on our surfboard – and our mind is still and at peace. At other times there are so many thoughts whirring around that we can't even pick up the mantra. The sea seems too rough to surf.

As we pay attention to our thoughts and accept them, we will find that they get quieter. Our thoughts, images and feelings only become a problem if we get hooked by them, if we get tempted to follow their lead. But we have a choice: we can either tag along with our thoughts or focus on our mantra. It is a free choice. If we know there are lots of things on our mind, it might be helpful as a preparation for meditation to sit quietly watching these surface thoughts for a while (*See Appendix II*). Sometimes naming them, when they interrupt our meditation, helps us to stay detached from them, not getting hooked by them: *work, shopping, friends etc.* Slowly, they get quieter, less demanding and we become aware of the gaps between the thoughts, which allow the mantra to sound uninterruptedly.

The tradition stresses the inevitability of thoughts: "A brother came to Abba Pastor and said: 'Many distracting thoughts come into my mind, and I am in danger because of them.' Then the elder thrust him out in the open air and said: 'Open up the garments about your chest and catch the wind in them.' But he replied: 'This I cannot do.' So the elder said to him: 'If you cannot catch the wind, neither can you prevent distracting thoughts from coming into your head." (Sayings from the Desert Fathers)

Acceptance of our thoughts as a natural part of ourselves allows us to be more accepting of the way things are in our ordinary life. We learn to accept life as it is, not as we would like it to be. We learn to become non-attached to our views as to how things ought to be. Rather than trying to constantly change our situation in line with our ideas and wishes, which is the urge of

the *ego*, we learn to accept the situation in which we find ourselves, and in doing so our suffering decreases. We then discover what we are giving up is perhaps something we only thought we needed or wanted: we are already complete in our true *self*. The energy released by this cessation of struggle then allows us to accept or creatively respond so that we come to the attitude expressed in the following prayer:

> *God, grant me the Serenity*
> *to accept the things I cannot change,*
> *Courage to change the things I can*
> *and Wisdom to know the difference.*

The mantra – one of the disciplines for one-pointed focus

Attention is the essence of meditation. Just as Christian meditation recommends repeating a prayer word, a mantra, all Wisdom Traditions propose a tool for detaching our mind from surrounding sounds, internal thoughts and feelings: watching the mind at work, building a particular visualisation, watching the breath, or repeating a mantra. These are in fact all equally effective ways of bringing the mind to single-pointed focus.[4]

There is an Indian story that illustrates the usefulness of aids to focusing:

Elephants are not as peaceful, wise and well behaved as often portrayed. If uncontrolled they will walk any which way, knocking

---

[4] We are so used to *multi-tasking* in our world that we find doing one thing at the time with full attention difficult. Piero Ferrucci in his book, *What We May Be*, gives several practices to enhance this ability of focusing scattered attention by using the senses imaginatively.

over things on their path. Whenever possible their mischievous trunk will pick up what it can – bananas, mangoes, anything tempting on all the roadside stalls.

Those who train elephants, the mahouts, are very aware of this fact. When they have to take an elephant through the crowded streets in a religious or marriage procession, they have two ways of controlling the elephant's behaviour. First they dress him in a special way with decorations and a seat on his back, making him feel important. This encourages the elephant to walk in a careful and measured way. Secondly they give his mischievous trunk a stick to hold on to and the elephant proudly holds on to this and is not tempted in any way to pick up tasty morsels.

Our mind is really like this elephant: if like the mahout we accept its wayward nature and develop strategies to deal with it rather than getting irritated and cross, we make the seemingly impossible possible. If we give the mind something to hold on to like a mantra, it too is not so tempted to follow its own inclinations and fancies and is less inclined to wander off.

The true nature of our mind is silence. Thoughts appear against this matrix of silence. When using a mantra, for instance, we focus on the word sounding in the silence and note the interruption caused by thought. Eventually the gaps get wider and slowly the mantra reigns supreme in the gaps, the doors to silence.

Thoughts and other distractions happen at the surface level

of our mind. But the effect of meditation is at a far deeper level. Our surface mind can be busy and yet our deeper self is calm. Often when getting up from a 'distracted' meditation we can still feel much more calm and peaceful, as long as we did not get irritated or critical with ourselves.

Whereas all of these disciplines are effective, the most effective way of stilling the mind can be a combination. When meditating purely by focusing on the mantra the mind may happily shift to *double tracking* – the mantra and the thoughts run side by side without any problem. But when adding awareness of breath and letting the mantra float on the breath, thoughts may soon disappear into the background. It seems the more we give our mind to focus on, the easier it finds it to let go of the endless stream of thoughts.

Christian meditation places a great emphasis on simplicity: all we need to do is just repeat our word. But we do not just repeat it; we say our word with attention and intention: we use our mind and our will. It is not a mechanical repetition but a longing call to the Divine to help us remember who we are in our essence. However, simplicity is difficult to accept for people of our times. We are used to having to learn complicated theory before we believe we can do anything really. But meditation is a revolutionary discipline: it will transform us and our habitual way of thinking, from complexity and fragmentation to simplicity and harmony.

Pernicious peace

There are various stages to mantra meditation. At first we are sounding the mantra in our mind silently, and then over time it seems we are listening to it and finally it seems to sound itself in our being.

This peaceful listening to the mantra can easily become what the Desert Fathers and Mothers called *the pernicious peace;* it can become a pitfall, in the same way as purely focusing on relaxing the body can be. Instead of being alert, awake and attentive, we start to float in the relaxation and the peace, as if in a light trance. The temptation is to let go of the mantra, as this seems a disturbance at this point. If we do, we will feel happy when we come out of meditation, but drowsy, slightly disconnected, instead of feeling energised and focused with clarity of mind after a disciplined meditation.

When we are in this state, images can also appear. Most of these are hypnagogic images: images that appear as we are nearing sleep. They are often really weird, as they come out of the dustbin of our mind. One meditator talked of the image of yellow boots marching by themselves past the window. Often these are accompanied by nonsensical phrases.

The way to deal with these hypnagogic images is to focus on our word with effortless attention and let them go back into the dustbin from whence they came. Seemingly significant ones at this stage are linked to isolated emotions at the border of our personal subconscious.

Single-minded attention

These tools to still the mind, such as using a mantra or watching the breath, all lead eventually to effortless one-pointed attention. All Wisdom Traditions generally recognise this as being the key to entering deep interior silence and stillness. We saw how the brain followed our lead and facilitated that.

Single minded attention, however, is not the same as willed concentration. A clear distinction is to be made between disinterested concentration and interested concentration: "A monk absorbed in prayer and an enraged bull is the one and the other concentrated. But the one is in the peace of contemplation whilst the other is carried away by rage. Strong passions therefore realise themselves as a high degree of concentration ... but it is not a matter of concentration but rather obsession ... True concentration is a free act in light and in peace. It presupposes a disinterested and detached will." (*Meditations on the Tarot*)

Interested concentration includes the emotions and implies an effort of the will with the aim of achieving something. If we ask children to concentrate they furrow their brow and we can see their body tensing up. They are trying to please us and achieve what we want them to achieve. Disinterested concentration is effortless and has an element of playing like a child.

We are then like a true tight-rope walker, totally in harmony and balanced, because he is one with the movement, as we are one with the mantra.

Without effort, by not trying, by not wanting to achieve anything, but by accepting what is, we focus totally on what is at hand. Then we reach a deep creative silence and become the silence: "Music heard so deeply that it is not heard at all, but you are the music while the music lasts." (T.S. Eliot) Silence in turn leads to knowledge of the true reality and the truth of our own being.

Having talked about all the ingredients necessary to allow the mind to come to stillness it is important to remember it is not just a question of following rules and precepts to arrive at the contemplative state. There is also an unconscious way of coming to wisdom:

On his very first visit to China a man was captivated by the beauty of jade. He felt driven to find out all he could about it. So he approached a Chinese friend to ask whether he could recommend a teacher. Fortunately for him his friend did know some one who could help. A few days later the man appeared on the doorstep of the recommended teacher. He rang the bell and after a few minutes he was admitted by a servant, encouraged to leave his fee in a basket and was shown to a room. This room was totally bare and painted white. There was one chair in the middle of the room with a small table next to it. After a few minutes the servant reappeared carrying a beautiful piece of jade that he placed on the little table. The man waited patiently for the teacher to appear. But no one entered the room.

After an hour the servant opened the door and showed the man out. The man was a little nonplussed, but yet he decided to go again. He thought that it was perhaps a test. He had heard about novices wanting admittance to a monastery being so tested.

Week after week the same sequence: the door opened, he was encouraged to leave his fee. After that he was shown into the room and a piece of jade was left next to him. The teacher never appeared. One day, however, everything seemed the same as always, but a few minutes after the servant had come in and left the jade, the man jumped up and stormed out and rang his friend at the first opportunity. When his friend enquired what had been so different this time to make him so angry, he exploded and told him: "It is unbelievable! I have had enough! The teacher still hasn't appeared! And on top of everything this time the servant left a fake piece of jade!"

CHAPTER THREE
Conditioned thoughts

A sense of oneness with the Divine can be experienced by anyone at any time when the body and mind are stilled. But for the effects of this experience to be fully integrated into our life, we need to understand how our ego is built up and how consequently we create a world of illusion out of our socially, psychologically and emotionally conditioned thoughts. Whereas during the actual periods of meditation we still the mind, at other times during the day reflection on thoughts and attitudes is essential.

We need to become aware of how we create images of ourselves, of the world and of God that prevent us from seeing reality as it is and how this tendency is driven by the primary survival needs. We need to become aware of our tendency to repress and project certain aspects of our personality for the sake of security and survival. By bringing unconscious conditioning and drives to consciousness, change becomes possible. We can then break out of this prison of the ego into the freedom of the self.

* * * * *

One of the qualities of the parietal cortex, which is associated with the *ego,* helps us to orient ourselves in time and space. This orientation inevitably involves needing to make distinctions and divisions; it creates a world of duality. It is interesting to note in this context that the Sanskrit word for *ego, ahamkara,* really means *aham*: "I am" and *kara:* "the action". This stresses therefore the connection between the *ego* and *doing.* Action too implies division, division between subject and object, the individual acting and the rest of creation acted upon: creating once more not only duality but now also possible conflict. The link between that and survival is very clear. Our early ancestors only survived in the dangerous environment in which they found themselves because of a strong survival instinct supported by the ability to plan and act intelligently. We are still influenced by this drive and carry this pool of memories in our consciousness in what Jung called *the collective unconscious,* and in our physical body in our genes.

The influence of genetic inheritance, however, is not as strong as first assumed. While the *Genome* project was progressing people speculated that everything would be found to have a genetic cause. Articles stressed that general intelligence and even personality qualities, such as openness to experience, conscientiousness, extroversion/introversion, neurotic traits, addiction and even the likelihood of divorce, were largely inherited, although some of these were previously generally assumed to be for the most part environmental. But when the project was finished, contrary to expectations, environmental factors were found to be very important. There were not as many significant genes as predicted and they were organized in a chaotic manner; they were not as efficiently arranged as once thought.

Therefore, the expression of our genetically determined instinct for survival will vary according to our environment and conditioning. In this respect the *ego*, our main instrument for survival, will change and adapt its tactics according to the pressures that surround us. It will suppress anything that threatens our continuation. All that we do on this level of consciousness is driven by this prime need. We adapt, behave and present ourselves in ways that secure our acceptance and survival.

Images of self

We are shaped and moulded by our past and the environment in which we find ourselves more than we at first realised. We think that our behaviour and most of our responses to the situations in which we find ourselves are based on our own free choice. Yet the fact is that many of our reactions are habitual, following an accepted code of conduct. We tend to deal with the world from within a matrix of complex survival conditioning that filters and colours the reality we see in many ways.

We adopt images, roles and attitudes expected of us as long as it means security. These may or may not accord with who we are at the deepest level of our being. To be acceptable, we even own images others have of us that are more based on their own emotional perceptions and ambitious expectations than our reality. We take the *ego* for the only centre of our consciousness.

We have consequently forgotten who we truly are at heart. *Who do you think you are?* We don't really know who we are. We consider our identity superficially. We are like Nasrudin in the Sufi story who went into a bank to cash a cheque. When he was asked to identify himself, he took out a mirror and peered into it and said: "*Yes, that's me alright.*"[1]   fasinating

The image we have of ourselves, the image we have of others and the world in which we live, alters constantly and is shaped by our ever changing thoughts and emotions; and not only our own thoughts and emotions, but often those of others we have unthinkingly made our own. We filter everything that happens to us through this closely woven net.

The Buddha starts the *Dhammapada* with the statement that all that we are is the result of what we have thought: "What we are today comes from our thoughts of yesterday, and our present thoughts build our life of tomorrow: our life is the creation of our mind."

From the moment we are born we have not only our parents' genetic heritage but we also absorb unconsciously the thoughts and even the emotional and psychological energy of our parents or carers. Their general state of mental and emotional health, their attitude to life, to the environment and their relationships is passed on so to speak with the mother's milk. We rely so much on

---

[1] Idries Shah, *The Hundred Tales of Wisdom*

conscious, mental learning that we forget how much we absorb unconsciously from the people closest to us. By the time a child is three years old, this field will already form the matrix out of which he or she may well act for the rest of their life.

Actions are either modelled on the parental example or shaped by the rejection of this pattern of behaviour. Siblings and their attitude to us also affect us deeply – some research suggests that this influence is even more important than that of parents. We are all aware of, and even joke about, how the choice of a life partner was influenced by our relationship with our parents or our ranking position with siblings. Peer groups shape us as well, often encouraging behaviour contrary to the norm of the parents. If smoking and drinking is one way of being accepted in a group, young people will go counter to their upbringing to be part of the *gang*.

Cultural conditioning and its associated images are equally unconsciously rooted in us. Only when we leave the culture and society in which we were raised and meet with different ones, do we become aware of their all-pervasive influence on our thoughts and behaviour. They determine what we find praiseworthy or blameworthy. Even the meaning we attribute to our life is often culturally shaped. Freud called constraints imposed by the conditioning in the family and in society the *super-ego*. To break this hold over our mind and be open to other interpretations requires a considerable conscious effort.

We are a collection of images, true and false. We look

unconsciously for a sense of identity in everything within us and around us – reactions of other people, our relationships, our thoughts, emotions and roles.

Contemporary neuroscience identifies a particular part of the left side of the brain, sometimes called "the interpreter", as the centre that fabricates a plausible but not necessarily true sense of identity.

Even false images fulfil their purpose: they too contribute to who we think we are. Thinking that we have a clearly defined self-image makes us feel in control and gives us a sense of permanence and security. We seem to be unaware of the illusory nature of any images, based as they are on ever changing conditions.

False images, however, can be destructive for our true being. The projection of certain flawed images and their associated energy will attract events and people that confirm this defective opinion we have of ourselves – a self-fulfilling prophecy. A striking example in this respect is having an image of oneself as a *victim*.

The obsession with images may cause many of our addictions. One reason an alcoholic may drink is to forget his own flawed self images. A shopaholic hopes to find the attributes of his/her ideal image and a workaholic is addicted to the image derived from the position held.

If we do not become aware of how early emotional and social imprints shape our image, behaviour and attitude to the world, we remain automatons with 'knee-jerk' reactions. Everything that happens is then coloured by our conditioned expectations. We are then prisoners of the past, prisoners of our own unmet needs, prisoners of the *ego*.

But we have the choice not to react in a habitual way. A by-product of meditation is an awareness of our wider being. We become aware of the possibility that the *ego* is not all there is to our consciousness. When we can hear the inner voice of the *self* rather than the chattering surface one of the *ego*, insights are afforded in the roots of our present conduct. Once we become conscious of these, we are one step closer to loosening the bonds that bind us. An attitude of detachment from the behaviour of the *ego* – a standing slightly apart – creates a gap between stimulus and response, a gap in which choices can be made as to how to react. We become aware of the fact that these blind responses were determined in a particular time and place and often are no longer relevant. This is real freedom. We *can* break through their relentless inevitability; the fixed template *can* be loosened, habitual defensive structures *can* be removed and a free creative response is possible.

Helpful questions to ask ourselves before reacting are: *Do I really believe this or is my mother/father/brother/sister speaking? Do I really want to do this or do I fear criticism or rejection?*

When we become initially aware of how our conditioned thoughts can totally determine the life we lead, we may feel that we are nothing more than a product of genetics and conditioning, in other words *nurture* and *nature*, and freedom seems a mirage.

But the important thing to keep in mind is that it is only the *ego* that is so affected; the *self* remains free.

Religious conditioning

One of the strongest forms of conditioning that interferes along the spiritual path is our religious upbringing as a child. If we were brought up in the Christian religion we may not have heard of spiritual disciplines other than liturgy, set prayers and reading scripture. Our feeling is that anything else is not prayer: *This isn't prayer as I was taught!*

The true meaning of the word religion is to *re-link* or *re-connect*. Religion is meant to reconnect us to our original self before separation from the Divine. Organised religion – especially the fundamentalist aspect of it – often does not see that as its main function but confines itself to morality. Emphasis is laid upon judgment rather than mercy and may be expressed in an authoritarian and dogmatic way. This allows the Church to exercise power and control over the worshippers. Disobedience, breaking the rules, is considered a sin, causing feelings of guilt. But the emphasis on leading a moral life on the material level, valid in itself, focuses on the *ego* and does not acknowledge our true spiritual nature. It therefore does not offer a way to access our original *self*.

It does try to offer a sense of security in these chaotic times; it tries to counteract existential fear by offering undisputable certainties. How great that need is demonstrated by the growth of fundamentalist movements in all religions. People find comfort in being told what to do and in not having to face the difficulty of personal responsibility and decisions.

This is the reason why some young people have become estranged from the Church of their childhood. There seems to be a great spiritual hunger, especially amongst the young. For some this need is still often satisfied within the established framework of religion, for others the early negative experiences of religion can be such a hindrance that we turn away from our religious roots. We look elsewhere for the spirituality we need and the confirmation of our own spiritual being.

It is unfortunate that we need nowadays to distinguish between religious belief and spirituality; religious belief is often restricted in our minds to accepting a set of beliefs, reserving spirituality for those who wish to *experience* the truth of these beliefs – in fact between the perspectives of the *ego* and the *self*. But the two are of course inseparable. At times it seems as if we have forgotten that all religions spring from one individual's spiritual experience, whether we are talking about Jesus, the Buddha or Mohammed.

Yet there is another dimension of religion and that is the experiential one "centred on man and his strength. Man must develop his power of reason in order to understand himself, his relationship to his fellow men and his position in the universe ... He must develop his powers of love for others as well as for himself and experience the solidarity of all living beings ... of oneness with the All ... Man's aim ... is to achieve his greatest strength. Virtue is self-realization." (Erich Fromm, *Psychoanalysis and Religion*) The emphasis here is on personal responsibility, connectedness, joy and peace. This dimension of religion presupposes the existence of our true *self.* This is the change in outlook that acceptance of meditation requires. It may well be difficult but is also intensely liberating.

Images of God

Part of our religious upbringing is our inherited images of God. These may well be a further hindrance to us on the spiritual path. We must become aware of how our ideas about God are not only shaped by social factors, but also are distorted by our conditioning, our personal fears, hopes and needs. They are often a product of our early childhood linked with our attitudes especially to parents and teachers.

The Christian scriptures show us a sequence of images of God linked to humanity's social evolution. First we meet the tribal God of the Old Testament: all-powerful, protective, bountiful, awesome but also distant, capricious and unpredictable, like nature on which small often migrating communities were so dependent. This is followed by a more impartial God, omnipotent and omniscient, not quite as distant, a just ruler like the ideal king the settled community or city state then required. Then we find the God of Love of the New Testament, reflecting the need for peace and service in a larger community, cementing relationships.

We have been made "in the image and likeness of God." (Genesis) But rather than understanding this as our having the Divine image and likeness within us, we take this literally and consequently we make God into our own conditioned image and likeness: "Most people are enclosed in their mortal bodies like a snail in its shell, curled up in their obsessions after the manner of hedgehogs. They form their notion of God's blessedness by taking themselves for a model." (Clement of Alexandria)

Often when we turn *agnostic* or even *atheist,* it is our image of God that has died. Nietzsche's cry, "God is dead," is a striking example of that. He no longer could accept the God of his childhood and threw out the baby with the bathwater.

Even if we know that we cannot encompass the Divine in words and thoughts, we find it too difficult to relate to something *unnameable, ineffable, and unlimited.* The human mind needs images – that is how it is made; it is part of our physical being in this level of reality of time and space. But we need to remember that God is much more than our images and we must look beyond the images to the Reality they point to. As a Buddhist saying underlines, they are fingers pointing at the moon, not the moon itself.

We tend to treat the image as the Reality, ignoring that it is merely a shadow of the real. We in fact make idols out of our images. But we need to smash these idols. Meister Eckhart (14th century German mystic) put this forcefully in his saying:

"Therefore I pray to God to rid me of god." This saying is very similar to the Buddhist saying: "When you meet the Buddha on the road kill him." It is the Godhead beyond our images that we are intimately linked with. Our images can prevent our awareness of this link.

Our spiritual growth is marked by and reflected by our changing images of God. We must therefore be careful not to tread on the images of others. John Cassian relates the story in his *Conferences* of a desert monk in the 4th century who was told to let go of his anthropomorphic image of God. He obeyed, but a little later we hear his cry of anguish: "Woe is me, wretch that I am! They have taken my God from me, and I have no one to lay hold of, nor do I know whom I should adore or address!"

Survival needs and self-image

The foundation of all our conditioning is *survival.* We are born as fragile beings in this material plane with certain inbuilt needs to secure our continued existence here. We have certain instinctual abilities to respond to these needs in others. Without these we would not stand a chance: they are a gift of the Divine to help us stay alive. Most psychologists agree that these are: *security, love, esteem, power, control and pleasure.* Initially as a baby and young child we cannot meet these needs ourselves; we depend on others to do so. We desperately need security, love and esteem to get us through the first few very dependent years. Social research has shown the devastating effect of children being deprived of this love of a constant carer in some state orphanages due to under funding. Despite being given a modicum of security these children did not thrive at all: it is essential for us to know we are loved and valued. If one adds to that the lack of any pleasure in our existence, the ability to survive can get very weak. The need for power and control over what happens to us and what form our life takes comes after this initial stage. Being shifted from pillar to post, put in situations without knowing why, makes us feel powerless and consequently valueless.

Unfortunately, even in a fairly normal setting these prime needs are often only partially satisfied due to the social and economic circumstances in which we are born or the limitations of our parents or carers. Or sometimes we feel unconsciously that these needs were unmet – the reason for it may be unfounded, but the important thing is that this is how it was perceived. This determines our view of ourselves and the world and shapes our emotional and psychological approach to life. Our whole life can be influenced by our ability or inability to deal with, or creatively respond to, this perceived lack.

If our upbringing was full of love, security and encouragement, we are likely to grow up self-confident, optimistic and with a healthy self-esteem. We feel at ease with the world and are able to love and be loved in return. However, the result of a loveless and critical upbringing is often a feeling that we ourselves were to blame in some way or the other for this situation: we were not good enough to be loved and protected. We then tend to reject ourselves in the way that we were rejected, have a low self-esteem, and suffer from insecurity, fear and guilt. Of course these are extreme examples and it is hardly ever as clear cut as this. The impact of a loving upbringing can be counteracted by the behaviour of siblings or the non-acceptance by a peer group for one reason or another; or the opposite may happen.

This basic emotional programming very much influences our relationships with others. It often seems that it is more important to us what a person has to offer than who they intrinsically are. If our survival need for love, for instance, was not sufficiently met, the driving force in our life is to find love. We repeat the actions we thought were partially successful for us as a child: being very well behaved and doing anything to please. This led in the past to receiving sporadic attention and approval, which is equated with love in our eyes.

But these actions were only appropriate then and no longer have the same effect. We have imposed the past strategies on the present situation. The result is quite different now. We are in a self-fulfilling prophecy: the ingrained attitude from the past is the belief that we were basically not worthy of receiving love. The projected energy of that conviction often attracts people with a similar psychological frame work. The result is that love has no chance to flourish nor the ability to form a loving relationship. We need to feel worthy of receiving love to be able to give love.

However, if being well behaved and trying to please was not effective in the past in getting the love we needed, we may have adopted an attitude of self-sufficiency: *you don't need and love me, so I will cope on my own.* Keeping to that pattern will result in an inability to believe in the possibility of a real loving relationship with anyone despite evidence to the contrary. Moreover the established pattern learnt in childhood is a familiar one and therefore is preferred, as it affords an illusionary sense of security.

The way forward is either meeting with a balanced loving person who sees our true worth and is willing to nurture the sense of our own value or, perhaps at the same time, turning within to discover the unconditional love at our centre. This then allows us to let go of our doubts about our own lovableness and allows us to see that not we but our environment was the significant factor. Feeling of value is essential in allowing us to accept ourselves as lovable. The needs of love, security and esteem are very closely interwoven. Only awareness, supported by the *self*, will help us to break these chains that bind us.

As adults we are perfectly capable of fulfilling our basic *survival* needs on our own, provided of course we are mentally and physically fit. However, by then the strategies we have developed in our early years have become quite ingrained. It has become a habit to look for the fulfilment of these needs outside ourselves in things and people surrounding us. This is the quest for happiness we are familiar with:

"What the world values is money, reputation, long life, achievement. What it counts as joy is health and comfort of body, good food, fine clothes, beautiful things to look at, pleasant music to listen to ... If people find that they are deprived of these things, they go into panic or fall into despair ... They are so concerned for their life that their anxiety makes life unbearable, even when they have the things they want. Their very concern for enjoyment makes them unhappy ... In so doing they are alienated from themselves, and exhaust themselves in their own service as though they were slaves of others. The ambitious run day and night in pursuit of honours, constantly in anguish about the success of their plans, dreading the miscalculation that may wreck everything. Thus they are alienated from themselves, exhausting their real life in service of the shadow created by their insatiable hope... thirst for survival in the future makes them incapable of living in the present." (Chuang Tzu - 4/3rd century BCE)

Often only when life has shown us the unpredictability of these external props, do we realise that money and power do not yield unchangeable security; status and reputation do not lead to permanent esteem. We need to listen to the advice from the spiritual tradition: "If men thought of God as much as they think of the world, who would not attain liberation." (Maitri Upanishad)

We need to appreciate the world and other people for their own sake. If they become means to an end, if we depend on them for the fulfilling of our survival needs, especially of esteem, power, control and pleasure they are a hindrance to further growth. Life can then become a vehicle driven by an unconscious compulsive hunger for what we thought we did not get – we are demonically possessed by these *unmet* needs.

Of course we do need a degree of love, security, esteem, power, control and pleasure in our life. The desire for that is quite natural. As adults we can fulfil these ourselves, especially if we turn within; we need to turn inwards towards the *self* rather than outwards. Then we *know and experience* that we are already unconditionally loved, esteemed and valued at our essential core. Our attitude becomes then one of balanced self-confidence; the fulfilment of partially met needs becomes a mutual nurturing in loving relationships.

Repression and projection

We saw that one of the integral functions of the *ego* was to orient us in time and space by making distinctions, allowing us to find our way in this material reality. Just by asking the question, "Who am I?", the *ego* distinguishes between us and not-us, the cause of all duality. In doing so it creates boundaries, not only boundaries in the external world, but also boundaries between us and the environment, between our mind and our body and even between different aspects of our personality.[2] Under the guidance of the *ego* our reality becomes one of polarity and inner and outer fragmentation; we see everything outside ourselves as opposite to and separate from us. Within ourselves we are divided into acceptable and non-acceptable facets, thus causing severe impoverishment of life.

This is done, however, by the *ego* to help us survive. Especially

---

[2] For more detailed explanations of this tendency to create boundaries see Ken Wilber, *No Boundary*

in the early part of our life we create boundaries by suppressing and disowning certain aspects of our personality that are not valued, are criticised and rejected by those we depend on for security.

Everything our environment taught us, often indirectly, to find unacceptable, is repressed and becomes in Jung's terms our *shadow*. But the more we emphasize the acceptable parts and suppress the unacceptable ones the stronger becomes the energy tied up in the *shadow*. The *shadow* can seem threatening, as in this Zen poem:

On a lotus leaf sits a frog,
legs crossed, hands folded, back straight,
motionless, deep in meditation.
Behind him rears up a huge snake. Does he know?
Does he not know? On the lotus leaf sits a frog,
legs crossed, hands folded, back straight, motionless,
deep in meditation – Watch out!

If we do not become aware of the contents of our *shadow* we may well be overwhelmed on occasion by a destructive explosion of these suppressed qualities and their associated emotions and desires. A usually placid person, for instance, who has been conditioned to find expressing anger unacceptable, may suddenly explode with inappropriate rage. Later he will apologize with the words: "*I don't know what came over me! I wasn't myself!*" still disowning this potential aspect of himself. A reaction in anger may well have been justified but suppression over time made the strength of it totally out of proportion to the actual cause. An emotional overreaction like this is always a good indication of a *shadow* aspect at work.

These deep-seated *shadow* reactions to life and other people can be just waiting for the appropriate stimulus to manifest themselves in often unexpected and exaggerated ways. Obsessions are another clear sign of suppressed drives and blocks.

When a reaction seems totally out of proportion to the actual present cause, we need to ask ourselves later: *"Is this a situation I have been in before?"* If we do this in a contemplative reflective way, often images of other similar incidents quickly arrive and we can see the pattern and escape.

One way we have of dealing with pressure building up is to get rid of these characteristics permanently by projecting them out onto others. However, we do this unconsciously. We do not know what we are doing. Projecting out facets of our personality perceived as negative, unacceptable and problematic has the added advantage that we can externalise the disapproval shown towards us, which we now share. We can fight the facets safely outside ourselves. Once projected out it is very difficult for us even to realise that these attitudes and emotions belonged to us. At that stage we really have forgotten that we too possessed potentially these qualities we see in others: "Projections change the world into the replica of our own unknown face." (Jung) In some way this is often the real cause of unaccountable likes and dislikes at one level and violent disagreements and wars at another level.

The *enemy* represents everything we were taught to hate and despise in ourselves.

Not only do *bad* qualities get separated out, but also *good* qualities. Often the aspects we admire in others are talents we too possess, but have not been allowed to explore and express due to upbringing. We project out these potential talents onto others, giving part of our energy, part of our soul away. This may work for a while, but often there comes a moment when we feel let down by those on whom we have projected our lost qualities – they can never live up to our impossibly high expectations. The relationship between the hero, the *guru* and their admirers and followers can be blighted by these projections. We tend to put them on a pedestal, seeing in them all we would like to be and then are shocked, when we find out they are just as 'human' as we are.

Moreover the personal *shadow* is our link into the *archetypal shadow* dwelling in the collective unconscious and its tendencies can therefore be amplified by this primordial pattern of energy. When we talk about integrating the *shadow,* we do not integrate the *archetypal shadow*, but only the personal experiences and memories that resonated with the *archetype*. We will explore this more when we look at the teaching of Evagrius Ponticus on what he called the *demons*.

Becoming aware of the negative side of our conditioning and how our *unmet needs* motivate our thoughts and behaviour can at first make us feel very flawed and much wounded. Often when being faced with the *shadow* after stilling the conscious mind we find this so daunting that we turn away from the journey. *"I was alright before! There was nothing wrong with me! Why should I face aspects of myself I have long ago got rid of?"*

But we must always remember that these insights come from our deeper *self*, our link with the Ultimate Reality, without criticism or judgement. These survival needs are not a *burden* we are responsible for but a *gift* that allows us to survive on this plane of existence. What we *are* responsible for is reflecting on and reacting to the insights given by our spiritual *self*. We are also responsible for being aware of these same needs and wounds in others. We need to listen and respond to them without judging – with empathy, support and understanding.

The actual experience of these suppressed emotions is important and may well be the first step in accepting this shadow aspect of ourselves. Rejected aspects in the shadow do need to be acknowledged and accepted. And more than that: they need be loved. This is the difficult challenge: to love them as well as all other aspects of ourselves. We do not find loving ourselves easy due to our conditioning. Jesus' command "Love your neighbour as yourself." (Mk 12:29-31) is one we find very difficult as we first need to love and accept ourselves before we can truly love our neighbour.

Jung felt, however, that loving and accepting our *shadow* was possible, as most of the *shadow* was *gold*. Merely by bringing these facets of our being to consciousness, by facing our *shadow,* by facing the *snake,* we release its pent-up energy and thus tame it. The resulting self-knowledge will lead to growth, as we integrate these facets creatively in our being.

Only ignorance of them will allow them to overwhelm and possibly destroy us. We must acknowledge and accept all our facets. Having said that, however, not all should be translated into action as some may well be counter to the morality of our particular culture and society.

All these distinctions we make between ego, shadow and self are actually artificial and illusory: there is no polarity in the true reality of our being, only complementary aspects. In the outer reality, opposites are part of the same field of identity: "Opposites produce each other, depend on each other, and complement each other ... life is followed by death; death is followed by life. The possible becomes impossible; the impossible becomes possible. Right turns into wrong and wrong turns into right – the flow of life alters circumstances and thus things themselves are altered in their turn." (Chuang Tzu) In fact, the things we perceive outside ourselves are really a projection of what is going on inside ourselves. And the things we experience inside us are really a projection of what is outside.

By getting in touch with our deep *self* that dwells in love, we are encouraged to leave this illusion of duality and fragmentation of our *ego* mind. We learn to acknowledge and accept all potential parts of our being and withdraw our projections one by one. In doing so, we recall these lost parts of our soul. Wholeness rather that fragmentation is the essence of our being. Since these projections come from the *personal unconscious* they can be *changed* by being made *conscious* through insight.

Changing the mould, breaking with conditioning represents a step into the unknown. This involves a radical change of perception. Any change is painful and requires courage, but if taken as an exciting, although difficult, challenge, it will be worth it, as it will <u>lead to growth and freedom</u>.

Destiny

Not all conditioning and expressions of *unmet needs* are necessarily negative. Our early conditioning can also shape us into the person we are meant to be. Each person is unique in his real *self* and has a role to fulfil in life and lessons to learn. This is beautifully expressed at the end of Plato's *Republic* in the myth of *Er*. Er died but came back to life to tell *what he had seen in the other world*. He talks about reward and punishment for deeds done on earth. Then the souls appear before the daughters of *Necessity* and are told the following: "Souls of a passing day, here begins another cycle of mortal life that leads to death. No Destiny shall cast lots for you, but you shall all choose your own Destiny ... They mostly chose according to their experience in their former life ... When, therefore, all the souls had chosen their lives ... they went in turn before Lachesis (the daughter of Necessity) ... she sent with each the Destiny he had chosen, to be his guardian through life and fulfill all his choices ... Then ... all travelled into the Plain of Oblivion ... drunk a measure of the River of Neglectfulness ... and forgot everything." The *guardian's* role is to remind them.

A similar belief can be found in the Hindu philosophy, where it is the *Rishis*, the wise sages, who look after humanity – similar in concept to the Buddhist *boddhisattvas* – and help the soul to choose even the parents and environment to facilitate the working out of Destiny/Karma.

In Christianity there is also a strong tradition of the concept of *calling* and *destiny* – we are called "by name." (Isaiah) Each one of us is unique and special. *Calling* always seems to suggest something grand, to do something special, but it can simply mean to be called to be who we really are, where we are, such as a good parent, empowering others to grow.

That deeper *self*, this guiding force within us, the meeting ground with the Consciousness of Christ within, we sometimes give the mythical form of our *guardian angel*. We need to listen to and follow this call of our true being.

We can access this guiding force and listen to the *small still voice* in different ways depending on our personality. There are as many ways of accessing the Divine as there are people. Work with the *Enneagram* – a system that divides humanity into nine distinct personality types – has emphasised that different personalities need different ways and environments to pray – as indeed has work with *Myers-Briggs* and other personality indicators. Meditation is only one way of getting in touch with the Divine, with the higher Reality – it is *a* way but not the only way.

Survival needs and roles and functions

The roles or functions we are given or adopt in society can also be a reflection of our *unmet needs* and conditioning. They can either be a positive expression of the qualities brought out in us by our conditioning that help us to fulfil our destiny or they can be proof that we are still prisoners of its negative aspects. In the latter case we still follow outmoded patterns of childhood. We are still trying to placate and please parents or society by doing what is expected of us rather than give expression to who we really are and unfold our innate gifts and talents, still seeing ourselves as others see us.

But it can be incredibly difficult, even traumatic, to have to go against the expectations of family, culture and environment. Sometimes the pain and unhappiness caused to others may mean that we may have to postpone what we feel is our real path, or possibly find a compromise for the time being. However, if the situation causes a debilitating dis-ease, painful actions may be absolutely necessary.

Erich Fromm in *Psychoanalysis and Religion,* quotes studies in which the conflict between the expected role and the innate wishes and abilities causes severe symptoms requiring specialist therapeutic help. In one case the father expected the son to follow in his footsteps and start working in his firm with the view to taking over the running of the business. The son loved theoretical physics and was very talented in that field. Yet the pressure of the father in the form of "promises, warnings and appeals to his sense of loyalty" resulted in him complying with the father's wishes. He was the only son and the father's health was failing. The conflict was so great that the son became clinically depressed as a consequence of his inability to assert himself and follow his own inner voice. The conflict between the *ego* and the *self* resulted in a crisis. Not living according to the promptings of our inner *self* and not unfolding our given talents can lead to either total repression of our feelings and a resulting lack of joy in life or a lack of integrity that can not be sustained for long. If 'wholeness' and integration of the *ego* and the *self* is to be achieved, independence and a feeling of self-worth are essential. If we have the courage to live our own destiny even those initially opposed will over time sense the truth and integrity in the situation and accept the change in direction.

Sometimes inner tension is a result of us going against the convictions coming from the *self,* and adopting an attitude prevalent in our society. A writer had accepted the generally held view that money and prestige were most important and had taken a well paid, prestigious job. After some time he started suffering from dizziness and headaches caused by having to write things that went against his own sense of integrity and conscience.

We can also damage our true being by exclusively identifying with one of the individual roles we play: teacher, accountant, doctor, parent, husband/wife, brother/sister, son/daughter, carer, nurturer, listener, advisor, friend – to mention just some of the positive ones. For each activity we adopt a separate *persona* or mask. These identifiable *personas* are important; they have to be recognisable and adapted to the society we live in. But instead of seeing these different *personas* as aspects of our total personality to be used in executing specific functions, we become entirely identified with one limited aspects of ourselves; we take that single aspect to be the whole. We focus on one facet of the diamond that is our true being rather than be aware of the whole jewel. This is especially so in the case of our occupations. We often totally identify with our profession. Society encourages this pigeonholing; people always ask what we do. Therefore there is a tendency to become what we do. We are a road sweeper, a painter, a lawyer, a mother, a teacher and so forth. This then spills over in the rest of our life. Even in our role as *father* for instance we wear the mask of the *business man*. We forget who we truly are:

A duck walks into a pub and orders a pint of lager and a ham sandwich. The landlord looks at him and says, "But you are a duck!" "I see your eyes are working," replies the duck. "And you talk!" exclaims the landlord. "I see your ears are working," says the duck, "Now can I have my beer and sandwich please?" "Certainly," says the landlord, "sorry about this, it's just we don't get many ducks in this pub. What are you doing round this way?" "I am working on the building site across the road," explains the duck. So the duck drinks his beer, eats his sandwich and leaves. This continues for two weeks.

Then one day the circus comes to town. The ringleader of the circus comes into the pub and the landlord says to him: "You are with the circus, aren't you? Well, just listen to this. I know this duck that would just be brilliant in your circus – he talks, drinks beer and everything!" "Sounds marvellous," says the ringleader, "get him to give me a call." So the next day, the duck comes into the pub. The landlord says "Hey, Mr Duck, I reckon I can line you up with a top job paying really good money!" "Sounds great, where is it?" says the duck. "At the circus," says the landlord. "The circus?" the duck enquires. "That's right," replies the landlord. "The circus? That place with the big tent? With all the animals? With the big canvas roof with a pole in the middle?" asks the duck. "That's right!" says the landlord. The duck looks confused. "What on earth do they want with a plasterer?"

If we are happy with our job, if it affords us esteem in the eyes of others and in our own eyes, all seems well. If society looks down on what we do and undervalues the contributions we make, our self-esteem can be correspondingly low. A good example of this occurred a few years ago when for political reasons, teachers in the UK were unfairly criticised and made scapegoats for a failing system. Due to adverse comments made in the media many felt undervalued, lost self-esteem and the enthusiasm for the job. They left the profession in droves.

When for some of us our professional life suddenly dramatically changes – we are made redundant or retiring age has come – the world may seem to come to an end, as our self-esteem and sense of value have been so dependent on this role. Or when children leave home, this again can have a devastating effect – the *empty nest* syndrome – when the woman has totally identified with her role as mother. If we are too attached to a specific function or role, we lead a dependent *ego* existence that revolves round external factors only. Losing this one aspect can feel like being unmasked with nothing real underneath. In these different roles we operate on the surface on parallel lines, rather than all aspects of our being converging on the one centre of the *self.*

Apart from a single identification we can also become very fragmented if we accept all the different *masks* but again lose sight of the whole. This tendency is reinforced by society, for instance, by telling us to leave our personal problems at home. We tend to fence off our different roles; we can even resent it if one area impinges on another. The result is that we perceive many different, even conflicting selves, many of them even false. A friend told me: "I don't really know who I am anymore. I am a different person, depending on whom I am with and what I am doing!" Then we are lost in *multiplicity* and in *alien images.* (Meister Eckhart)

Others have never lost the wider view of their personhood.

They were always aware of their different possible roles without letting one or the other overwhelm and dominate. They were basically free. When one role fell away they could transfer the energy and enthusiasm to other innate talents, which were until then perhaps inevitably neglected.

We need to keep some distance between who we are and what we do to avoid this total identification with the *ego*. Being somewhat detached from our roles and actions does not devalue the importance of that particular expression of our being. It allows us to keep things in perspective and actually helps us to do these tasks better, as we do them for their own intrinsic value. By not wanting to own what we do for our own *needs*, we are able to act in the world in a poised manner, ready to do purely what the need of the situation demands. We are then intrinsically free, free of all limited needs and desires. Our acts are then our free gift to the world. We behave totally in accord with our spiritual nature: "Yet not I, but Christ lives in me." (St Paul) Then there will be no veils hiding us from our true *self*. We act and stay "in this present moment free and empty ... truly unimpeded by any images ... united and in harmony within, like the sound of a major chord." (Meister Eckhart)

Being wounded is inevitable. That is our human state and cannot be avoided. But we do not have to be a victim of unconscious drives, of circumstances, caught between the guilt of the past and fear of the future. With courage and by practising awareness, we can transform our thoughts and hence our reality and thus unfold the whole of our being. This is *the* essential task we have to face:

"What can we gain by sailing to the moon if we are not able to cross the abyss that separates us from ourselves?" (Thomas Merton)

CHAPTER FOUR

The interplay of the ego and the deeper self

Now that we have explored the conditioning and the role 'survival needs' play, we need to become consciously aware of how these unconscious drives mould our behaviour. We can only be detached from the influence of some 'need' when we understand it clearly.

We need to become aware of the interplay between the ego and the self: the ego resisting and the self encouraging. The ego wants to keep us safe on the surface, maximising our chances of survival. This is easiest to see clearly in the resistances we put up to the discipline of meditation.

* * * * *

We need to keep in mind constantly that we are much more than a mind filled with thoughts, feelings, desires and needs. It is only the tip of the iceberg of our whole identity. This surface identity, our *ego*, is based on *doing*, determined by conditioning in all its forms. We need to remain aware of the games the *ego* plays and realise their origin.

The identity of the deeper *self* is based on *being*. In the silence of meditation we become ever more conscious of the deeper *self* as the pull that unaccountably keeps us searching, that helps us to persevere. This deeper aspect is pure consciousness and yet an individual one, unaffected by action and environment. Its reason for existing is purely that it exists. It is free of content, linked into a realm beyond time and space.

The *self* cannot control the *ego* directly, but it can influence developments by reminding us of the wider reality in which we are embedded. It furnishes the insights needed just at the time when they are needed, when we are ready to deal with them. We are never given more than we can cope with at any one time.

Slowly over time the *ego* gets less frightened, sees that the change is a change for the better and allows our spiritual nature to inform our behaviour. The stages of our journey are punctuated by our insights into the restrictions of the *ego* and the growing awareness and pull of our *self*.

Slowly the seemingly polar opposites become complementary aspects of one integrated being. When dealing with the difficulties on our path, we must never lose sight of the fact that to connect with our spiritual side, leading to wholeness and integration, is something we are meant to do.

Resistance by the ego

The moment we start to meditate the *ego* goes into action. It does not like us entering the level where we will meet the *self*, where we will be out of its total control. It is the survival expert and wants to keep us in its own sphere of influence. It is like an over-protective parent, wanting to keep the child safe and close by, not allowing it to develop and learn independently. But to grow we need to leave and make our own home. In the same way insisting on going into the silence and going under the waves of thoughts is initially like a painful leaving home, only to find the peace and joy of arriving at your *true* home.

The reason the *ego* plays these games and strongly resists the pull to silence is that it fears change; change implies different survival tactics. The *ego* has spent the whole of our childhood perfecting our responses to secure our continued existence and is quite happy for us to continue this way. But we have seen how most of our habitual responses are now out of date.

When we try to take the plunge into silence, the *ego* will emphasise and increase *awareness of thoughts* as a barrier to going deeper. It encourages us to identify with these surface thoughts and emotions. Their mad dance is meant to drive us to distraction, and to despair, so that we assume meditation is not for us. And yet, if we persevere, gaps will appear between our thoughts – doors to enter the silence.

Even the peace and silence we then reach becomes a way in for the *ego* to tempt us by encouraging us to let go of the mantra.

We may convince ourselves that the mantra disturbs the peace after we enter a light pleasant trance, the *pernicious peace*. We then tend to forget the world, ourselves and our journey. Thus the *ego* has hindered our progress.

But if we manage to hold onto the mantra, the *ego* may whisper to us: *Isn't this boring, just repeating a word? What a con! Variety is the spice of life! Don't just sit there, do something!* It wants us to go off and forget this journey in frenetic activity, amusement and work. Yet meditation is a revolutionary discipline that asks us to do the opposite: *Don't just do something, sit there.* We are encouraged to stay faithful to one thing only.

If we are still meditating but finding it difficult, the *ego* might try a different approach, playing on our need for diversity, prompting us to consider: *Are you sure that this is the right method or the right mantra? Shouldn't you change your mantra?* By encouraging us to chop and change again the *ego* is making sure we are not going anywhere.

If the *ego* has failed to hinder our progress thus far, it might well try a final approach, prompting us to wonder: *The teacher really could be more inspiring! The group is really not very supportive, should I look elsewhere?* And off we go on our restless search. Sometimes a change may be right, especially in the beginning, but often it is avoiding the real work of becoming aware.

Thoughts like: *This is self-indulgent; we should do something useful for others instead* often appear. This has often been the accusation thrown at contemplatives. But meditation allows us over time to act from our deeper *self* where we are connected to everyone and everything. As we change, we are healed and integrated, and so we affect other people: "Acquire inner peace and thousands around you will find salvation." (St Seraphim of Sarov)

I am sure we have all met at some time or other these ploys of the ego to keep us on the surface.

Resistance due to religious conditioning

If we were brought up in a strict denominational religion where different ways of prayer were frowned on, we may well find that in following the path of meditation we feel disloyal to our parents. This either stops us in our tracks or we continue our own search but feel divided within ourselves.

Many of our religious images can be a real hindrance on the path. If we are brought up with 'God, the Father' and our experience of our own father was far from nourishing – we felt rejected, criticised, abused – this image will not give us the trust needed on the spiritual path, as our self-image is one of being totally unworthy of God's attention. Even calling and thinking of God as *Mother* does not really deal with this problem – we are merely replacing one image with another. Other people may have had the same rejecting experience with their mother.

If we are brought up with the image of an old man sitting on a cloud in heaven, and we have a scientific bent, soon the thought occurs that this is just impossible – religion becomes outdated childish make-believe. If God is seen as a judge, he becomes someone to avoid rather than relate to, as so many of us carry such a burden of perceived guilt.

Resistance through unmet needs

At this stage we also need to be aware of the way our *ego* will try to deter us from the silence of meditation by playing the old emotional *unmet need* tapes with their flawed self-images.

If our *love* need was not met or we have only experienced conditional love – love as a reward for good behaviour – it may be hard for us to imagine that God, which is Unconditional Love, is also there for us. The *ego* taunts with: *You know you are unlovable! God can't unconditionally love you! This is for other people, not you!* Meditation is based on a loving relationship of faith and trust with the Divine. Our sense of unworthiness might make entering into that relationship initially very challenging.

If our *security* need has not been met this may well lead to an urge to control the immediate environment, other people and situations. As we fear being out of control – control equals security – the *ego* plays on this particular weakness: *Are you sure this is a good idea? You won't be in control! Are you not frightened?* The *letting go* that meditation requires may be therefore at first incredibly threatening.

If a need for *esteem* is our driving force, which makes us put excessive emphasis on status and reputation, then to consider doing something *unorthodox*, such as meditation, may not fit the real need to be accepted and respected.

If we did not feel valued, as the pattern of our early life was marked by being ignored, with our own opinions not asked for or taken on board, then to trust in our own inner voice would be a problem.

The way forward is to remind ourselves that all these emotions are based on our conditioned attitudes formed in the past. Therefore we can learn to switch the tapes of and not listen to these messages from the *ego*.

The pull of the self

The desire to believe in something beyond ourselves does not therefore come from the *ego*; it is the deeper aspect of our consciousness, our *self*, that is the attracting force. The pull of the deeper *self* makes us seek true meaning beyond everyday reality: "Among all my patients in the second half of life, that is to say, over 35, there has not been one whose problem in the last resort was not that of finding a religious outlook on life." (C.G. Jung, *Modern Man in Search of a Soul*)

Although Jung dealt with people when their problems had already developed into neuroses, his statement holds true for all of us. Considering that it takes time for neuroses to become so crippling that treatment needs to be sought, this awareness of a lack of spiritual values can start much earlier. He talked about *a religious outlook* because of the time he lived in, but I would now call it a *spiritual hunger*: a basic "desire for light and an irrepressible urge to rise out of primal darkness." (C.G.Jung, *Dreams, Memories and Reflections*)

Suppressed memories

Another reason the *ego* does not want us to get in touch with the deeper layers of our consciousness is that it has deposited there in the first layer, in our *personal unconscious*, any experiences that threatened our survival. But to transcend our *ego* we first have to descend there and face these forgotten painful experiences with courage.

The *ego* will question the validity of meditation at this point: *What is the point if I feel worse afterwards?* We need to ignore its encouragement to: *Let the past be! What is the point of reliving these experiences; they are better left alone!*

When we enter the forest of unconsciousness in the silence of meditation, we meet both the beauty and the beast: both forgotten memories of beautiful moments and painful ones. The emotions linked to this repressed material rise to the surface too: joy bubbles up, peace reigns, tears flow unexpectedly. Feelings of anger and irritation come to the fore. But these are the tears we did not cry when we were hurt; this is the anger and irritation we felt at a time when we could not express them. We need to allow them to come to the surface and be released.

We need to face the truth of these suppressed painful memories contain and learn from them. Just by bringing them to consciousness we can be healed. They will dissolve by us facing them squarely with or without the help of psychotherapy. There is not always the need to know the causes of these emotions. The saying: *just name your demons and your heart will tolerate them better* is very true.

The most important part of this process is acknowledging and lovingly accepting everything that comes up. These suppressed emotions are kept locked in our body. But this suppression requires an enormous amount of energy, causing tension and an obstruction to the general flow of energy. Therefore just the release of this buried energy is very healing. It has been trapped in our being for years as frozen emotions, blocks of ice; all we need to do is hold them up to the Light and Compassion of the Divine and they will melt.

In the same way that we habitually ignore the body we tend also to suppress our emotions, both in public and even at times in private. An important step is therefore to avoid adding to this store in the *personal unconscious* by becoming aware of our emotions, sensations and the reactions associated with them as they arise. Acknowledging emotions, being conscious of them, does not mean having to act them out in either words or deeds. The energy associated with unexpressed strong emotions can be channelled in different directions: physical exercise or creativity.

A clear sign of something stirring in the depth and the *ego* resisting is the feeling of boredom, dryness and pointlessness during meditation, often strongest just before a breakthrough will occur. Trust and persevere; trust that we are not alone in this but are accompanied every step of the way by our spiritual *self*, nourished by the Cosmic Spirit.

Remember that what happens in meditation is at a much deeper level than our rational consciousness. Our surface mind may be distracted, but at the same time healing takes place at the level our rational mind cannot reach, at the level of silent communion with our deep consciousness and the Ultimate Consciousness.

The role of therapy

If the wound was of a traumatic nature – abuse and abandonment – therapy may be useful for a time. A distressing experience threatens survival in the ego's view and it is suppressed, separated out and ring fenced. This suppression does not allow the experience to be digested. Only when traumatic experiences have been understood and we accept our woundedness, can that part of our being be re-integrated and absorbed in the wider personality, allowing growth to occur.

There are times when meditation may be possible only when the practitioner is accompanied by an experienced meditating spiritual director or a transpersonal psychotherapist. This may well be advisable for people suffering from severe clinical depression or severe neuroses. Their consciousness is already flooded by emotion and the surfacing of further emotions may tip the balance, unless they are helped to insight and understanding. Those suffering from an impaired or severely fragmented *ego,* as in multiple personality disorders, would be well advised to seek psychiatric help as accompaniment to meditation.

Other problems may also benefit from professional help for a while. But we have to go about this in such a way that it helps and does not hinder us on the path. Care needs to be taken to find the right therapy. Ken Wilber stresses in his book, *No Boundary,* that the level of our being at which the problem occurs will require different psychotherapeutic approaches.

Erich Fromm makes furthermore an important point in his book, *Psychoanalysis and Religion.* He distinguishes two different approaches: "psychoanalysis which aims primarily at *social adjustment* and psychoanalysis which aims at the *cure of the soul.*" In the first instance the aim is to make the person's behaviour conform to generally approved social and cultural standards and in the second the therapist is concerned with the individual developing his total human potential. Often a combination of the two is needed. But on the spiritual path the emphasis needs to be on *cure of the soul.*

An added difficulty to the quest to find out, "What made me the way I am?" pursued in analysis, in psychotherapy or in encounter groups is that often only one part and not the whole of our personhood is the focus, emphasising fragmentation rather than integration. Our quest for answers, reliving the experience in detail, can have an imprisoning rather than a freeing effect.

Analysis, if pursued in the wrong way, can lead us to feeling more insecure and more anxious. We can become quite spellbound by our earlier story and the games the *ego* plays. We keep digging to find the causes and spend years away from our journey. It can also lead to blaming others and evading personal responsibility by living in the past and not facing up to reality now. The *ego* would be quite happy if we were so distracted from our real aim, which is self-knowledge in the service of self-transcendence. We turn our back on spiritual growth in life:

The centipede was capable of running very fast. One day it was asked, 'How can you keep all your feet under control, never getting them crossed, never stumbling? At such speed too! And with what leg do you actually start to run?'

The centipede began to think and found he did not know. He went on thinking, trying to find out, but to no avail. He died on the spot, still busy thinking 'how?' and incapable of moving!

CHAPTER FIVE

The worldview – old and new

We need to look at one final layer of conditioning before we explore other ways of becoming aware of our motives. What makes changing our attitude so difficult is the powerful pressure of the prevailing view of reality that forms the mental background to our life. This has important consequences for our opinions and behaviour, especially now as we are at a period of transition from the Cartesian worldview to the one based on quantum theory.

The shift in scientific thinking necessitated by quantum theory was so revolutionary that even now 100 years later it has not really caught on. The old materialistic Newtonian paradigm still rules society as a whole. A consequence of this needed shift in perspective will be to accommodate the mind-set that allows us to become aware of our connectedness to the whole of the cosmos. This involves also accepting different levels of reality, including the spiritual dimension of our own being, the self, beyond the ego.

* * * * *

The *ego* is not only so dominant because of the powerful survival instincts that drive it, but also because of the fact that the prevalent worldview of scientific materialism supports and encourages this one-sided emphasis on the *ego* and the rational mind. Unless we understand that the worldview that surrounds us is not the only possible interpretation of reality, we are imprisoned by its restricted view. It won't allow for other ways of relating to reality and, even more damaging, ridicules those views.

Dualism versus unity consciousness

This scientific materialistic view is primarily dualistic. The origin of this attitude and its corresponding split between spirit and matter, between body and mind, between humankind and God is to be found already in the thoughts of the early Greek philosophers. But side by side with this dualistic view we find also the opposite view of a basic unity underlying everything, similar to the viewpoint expressed in *Perennial Philosophy.*

Plato's philosophy is in line with the *Perennial Philosophy* and supports the existence of the *self.* He believed in a transcendental reality, the home of the eternal Forms, to which we humans could relate, as there was something innate in our soul, the *nous,* our intuitive intelligence, which made us truly human and allowed us communion with this realm. This ability to see beyond the transience of the world could be accessed by contemplation and a spiritual/moral practice that purified the emotions. The material world was considered to be a mere shadow of the real. The senses were viewed as unreliable because of their link with the material body.

⚹ ⚹ For many centuries the philosophy of Plato informed the dominant worldview in the West. Over time it was explained and developed and thus made compatible with the Christian view of reality by later followers of Plato, the so-called *neo-Platonists,* such as Proclus and Plotinus in the 3rd century. They and their followers influenced many of the early Christian thinkers, including Origen, Evagrius, the Desert Fathers and St Augustine. Platonic ideas were further reinforced when Pseudo-Dionysius, a neo-Platonist, was translated in the 9th century. The latter was particularly influential as he was considered – mistakenly as it turned out – to be a disciple of St Paul.

Things changed during the Middle Ages with the translation of Aristotle into Latin during the 12th century; his ideas dominated the Middle Ages. This coincided with the emerging curiosity of wealthy secular people about the world they lived in.

⚸ Aristotle disagreed with Plato's view of reality. He did not believe in the prior existence of the Forms in a higher reality. He stressed the primacy of sense perceptions and considered forms and ideas as abstractions made by our own mind. His emphasis on the rational mind and the evidence of the senses, his scientific approach, spoke to the people of that time and to subsequent generations. His rational scientific view of reality was brought once more to the fore by Descartes and Newton in the 17th century and has prevailed till our time.

His rational scientific approach was often met with deep suspicion by theologians and Church authorities alike. St Thomas Aquinas, however, tried to reconcile Aristotelian thinking and Platonic theology by limiting each to their own sphere of competency, stressing that they were both of value but dealt with different realms of reality. The factual explanation of the natural world could be described by reason, but the higher reality giving meaning and purpose to all could only be accepted through intuitive faith. The two approaches could therefore exist peacefully side by side and appreciate the findings of each. But apart from Aquinas' brave attempt, both parties felt on the whole that they alone had the ability to describe reality in its totality. Instead of seeing these two approaches both as valid and complementary, being able to enrich each other by offering different interpretations of the same reality from different angles, they were progressively seen as polar opposites. The more one end of the pole got valued the greater the apparent conflict became, especially as emotions got involved.

It was considered on the whole that science could throw helpful light on religious beliefs but religion itself had nothing to offer in elucidating reality. The result was that rationality and intuitive intelligence were arraigned on different sides of the spectrum with damaging results for our culture and society: "The intuitive mind is a sacred gift and the rational mind is a faithful servant. We have created a society that honours the servant and has forgotten the gift." (Albert Einstein) The result is that we have ended up with knowledge, and we have lost wisdom. Over the following centuries, right up to our time, the mere concept of spiritual and intuitive faculties and even the existence of God was denigrated as unscientific and mocked as a primitive left-over from our past.

The Cartesian worldview and its consequences

Descartes was a mathematician who saw mathematical rules governing all of creation. These formed the structure to everything, the universe including our bodies. Moreover, he saw nature as divided into the realm of the mind: *res cognitans* and the realm of matter: *res extensa*. He viewed the human mind as totally separate – separate from our bodies, from the rest of humanity and creation. In fact, we are in his view isolated observers of the rest of the visible universe. The only thing we could be sure about was our capacity to think – our only real proof of existence: *cogito ergo sum* ("I think therefore I am"), linking existence firmly with thought.

Newton shared this dualistic and mechanistic viewpoint. He saw the universe as obeying certain mechanical laws. Once set in motion, creation obeys these rules inexorably with predictable outcomes. There is no innate creativity and freedom for the universe or the individual. The Newtonian Universe is therefore merely a great machine, hence the phrase *The Clockwork Universe*. Later interpreters even drew the conclusion that God's input wasn't really needed, perhaps only in starting the ball rolling. This led to a belief in an absent God busy somewhere else in the Universe, or even the feeling that God did not exist at all, exemplified by the cry of Nietzsche, "God is dead!"

This same deterministic, mechanistic approach was then extended to human beings. The English philosopher John Locke (17th century), like Aristotle before him, stressed the importance of the senses in shaping the human mind – he saw the human mind as a *tabula rasa* ("an empty slate") at birth. Identity is purely a function of sense impressions stored in the memory and our reflection on them.

The idea of humankind as no more than a mechanism surfaces in the early 20th century as behaviourist psychology. An example of this attitude can be found in O'Brien's statement in George Orwell's, *1984*: "We create human nature. Men are infinitely malleable."

But the point that was ignored over time was that none of the above great thinkers ever doubted the existence of God or humankind's link with the Divine. Descartes had both a clear intuition of himself as a thinking being and of God as a perfect entity influencing his mind. The *mind* of a human being was enlightened by God and therefore our insights and the mathematical laws were divinely inspired. Kant's idea that we filter and organise our experiences of the world through the concepts innate in the human mind, is very similar. Stress on innateness implies the Divine at work. Newton believed the Universe to be a body – not a machine – pervaded by God. Belief in God is the basic assumption underlying all of their work.

By accepting this mechanistic, reductionist approach, we humans start to feel valueless and powerless. We feel a mere product of our environment and an uninvolved observer of the rest of creation, not part of the whole cosmic process at all. This can give rise to a sense of alienation, isolation. These feelings then often express themselves in violence: an impoverishment of our true humanity.

Feelings of being disconnected and separate from nature have encouraged an attitude of treating the world as a mere object, even leading to a violent, dominating, exploitative stance, as exemplified by Sir Francis Bacon (17th century). Bacon claimed that nature had to be "hounded in her wanderings, bound into service and made a slave." She was to be "put in constraint" and the aim of the scientist was "to torture nature's secrets from her." It is not difficult to see here the beginnings of the despoiling of our planet.

Additional fragmentation has occurred from changes in society since the 19th century's industrial revolution, which accelerated after World War II. The sense of community that had existed till then, in which we were mutually responsible and interdependent – with the Church holding the answers to the meaning of life – has changed dramatically. From working with people we knew from childhood in our community, we moved to finding jobs elsewhere – often in the cities with the isolated individual responsible for his own survival and his own meaning.

The Church no longer had the same relevancy for some.

Unsupported and alienated we depend on our wits, jostling with everyone else for survival, in the Darwinian mode of *survival of the fittest*. This leads to the cult of individualism, manifested in the selfish attitudes of "I am alright, Jack!" and the viewpoint of *nimbyism* ("not in my backyard"). Qualities related to isolated individuals jostling for survival are highly rewarded: power, control, aggressive assertiveness, determination, striving for status, achievement, material gain. We can see the *ego* and the survival needs at work. Qualities of the self such as honesty, integrity, loyalty, truthfulness and friendship are often overruled. This materialistic viewpoint encourages us to take our surface personality, the *ego*, with all its apparent limitations and flaws for the whole of our personhood.

We are encouraged to think that the physical reality around us is the only reality and that beyond this there is nothing else; moreover, the boundary of our skin separates us from everything else. We feel alone and isolated. Consequently the fundamental feature of many people of our time is this sense of not being of lasting value, a lack of self-confidence or the other side of the coin – in compensation – over-confidence sometimes bordering on arrogance. Sometimes this can lead to a lack of responsibility for our actions and the effect they have on others and our environment.

Yet we feel instinctively that there is something lacking, but we don't know what it is that is missing. The fact is of course that there is nothing missing. We have been encouraged to just forget the existence of the spiritual aspect of our nature dwelling in the deepest level of our being, our *self*. We feel incomplete; there is emptiness within; we are not at home with ourselves and therefore also alienated from others. We look unsuccessfully outside ourselves for things and people that will make us feel complete, that will make us feel whole, yet all the time the remedy lies within. We need to get in touch with our spiritual nature, which at our deepest level connects us with everyone else and with all of creation. "*We are islands in t*he sea, separate on the surface, but connected in the deep.*" (William James, *Varieties of Religious Experience*)

The new worldview and its consequent connectedness

Quantum theory sees everything and everyone as interconnected and interdependent; all humankind is integrally and actively involved in the cosmic process. But we have not really accepted this yet: mainstream thinking is still that of the old worldview. Everything on the whole is still treated in a mechanistic and reductionist way. The reason for this lies in the difficulty of really understanding quantum theory and the impossibility of drawing firm conclusions because of its *uncertainty principle*.

Many scientists are therefore unaware of its wider implications for science or are struggling to incorporate these new ideas into an existing conventional framework. They still stress rational consciousness and deny the importance of intuition, although Albert Einstein stressed its significance in his statement: "the really valuable factor is intuition and the cosmic religious experience is the strongest and noblest driving force behind scientific research." As our worldview leads us to respect the opinion of scientists we are very much under their influence.

However, understanding the discoveries of quantum theory *is* important for everyone. The beauty of the subatomic world is that nothing has meaning or substance just in itself. All – including the human mind, body and spirit – are part of an infinite ocean of energy, patterns within patterns, relationships within relationships. Instead of being isolated depending on our *ego* qualities only, we are part of the whole.

All are integrally connected and supported by a vast underlying ocean of energy. Quantum scientists call this energy field the *Zero Point Field.*

Experiments had right from the beginning proved the existence of this connecting principle, this energetic force, but it was ignored as irrelevant to practical applications of this science and left out of the equations. Now scientists interested in the philosophical implications of quantum theory are drawing attention to it.

Research has proved that electrons are in perpetual motion constantly interacting with other particles and with this underlying field of energy.

If constant movement and interchange is true for electrons, then this is true for our energetic being as well. Basically we are made up out of atoms and their essential constituents, electrons. We too are packets of quantum energy interlinking and exchanging information in this sea of energy.

The particle and the wave

The reality discovered by quantum theory could be used as an analogy to explain the concept of different aspects of our wider nature. Experiments have shown that a subatomic particle, an electron, exhibits both *particle* like properties and *wave* like properties depending on the experimental set-up with which we examine reality: "We have to remember that what we observe is not nature itself, but nature exposed to our method of questioning." (Heisenberg) *NB*

Not only the experimental set-up but also the consciousness *NB* of the observer is important: "Subatomic particles existed in all possible states until disturbed by us – by observing or measuring – at which point, they'd settle down, at long last, into something real. Our observation – our human consciousness – was utterly central to this process of subatomic flux actually becoming some set thing." (Lynne Taggart, *The Field*)

Since *we* are made up out of electrons, we could take this as also applying to us. Given the *circumstances* we find ourselves in, metaphorically speaking, we either exhibit our *particle* nature or our *wave* nature. When we are about our daily business we identify with our *particle* nature; we are in our physical manifested *matter* aspect, ruled by the *ego* – separate, jostling for survival. When we enter the inner solitude and silence, we connect with our *wave* nature, our *self*, and through that with the *wave* reality of all humankind, creation, the Cosmos, the Divine.

Experiments of quantum theory either determine the *position* of a particle or its *momentum* – its speed and mass, but not both together. In the same way our *consciousness* can fix us either in our *particle* nature or emphasise our *wave* nature. We can either be frozen in time or in a state of flowing change. When we are concerned with questions: *What are we like at this particular moment? What is our position in life? What do we look like?* – we restrict our being and consciousness to our *position*. We take a freeze frame of ourselves; we are in our *particle* nature focused on our separate surface personality, judging and evaluating. However, when our consciousness is not engaged with particular thoughts but reflecting on questions of meaning and purpose: *Where do I come from? Where am I going? What is the pattern and meaning of my life?* – we are focusing on underlying connections, on the continuing motion of space/time; we are in our *wave* nature. When we are in this aspect of our nature we *know* intuitively, we make instinctive connections and seem even to be able to communicate over distance. In quantum theory experiments have shown that when we observe the *wave* aspect of reality, pairs of electrons that were close together in the beginning but have separated over time can still influence one another over vast distances.

The effect we have therefore does *not* stop at our skin, but our consciousness and that of every one else extends and is integrally connected with the rest of humankind and with this field. Awareness is woven throughout the structure of the universe: "deep down the consciousness of mankind is one." (David Bohm) Humanity and its actions are intimately involved with and co-responsible for the whole Cosmos. This worldview makes us profoundly aware that we too have a deep significance and meaning. Like all the atoms in creation we too are part of the Cosmic Dance. The Buddha too illustrated this truth of interconnectedness:

"In the heaven of Indra, there is said to be a network of diamonds, so arranged that if you look at one you see all the others reflected in it. In the same way each object in the world is not merely itself, but involves every other object and in fact is everything else. In every particle of dust there are present Buddhas without number." (Avatamsaka Sutra)

If we really take this thought on board, we also need to keep in mind that our every action, desire and thought has an effect on the whole. Each one of us is therefore an important aspect of the whole and personally responsible for the health of humanity, creation and the cosmos as a whole.

This new worldview implies therefore that we are much more than just an isolated, individual identity: the ego clinging to its separateness. It is only one complementary aspect of our personhood with another essential part of our being, our deeper self connected with everything else in creation forming the other one.

The turning point

The new worldview in which everything is part of an interconnected web of relationships resonates with the *Perennial Philosophy*. It also supports spiritual disciplines that presuppose different levels of reality, such as meditation.

PLATO

The turning point, the shift in perspective from the old to the new worldview, from the surface to the depth, however, is often not so much informed by the mind as by the heart.

With our mind we have turned away, but our heart retains intuitively the memory of our true *self*. We stay on the surface, but yet intimations coming from the *self* that there is more to life than we are experiencing at present come to the fore. The result is doubt, a vague feeling of dissatisfaction and of unease. Questions like: *Is there a reality beyond the one I can see with my ordinary senses? Who am I really beyond all the roles and masks life has given me? Why am I here? What is my meaning and the meaning of life?* – come to the fore. Sometimes we are consciously aware of these questions and sometimes they motivate our search from a deeper, unconscious level.

At one level we do know that we are much more than just producers and consumers. We do know there is no real enduring satisfaction or ultimate meaning in being a workaholic or a shopaholic, despite the saying "I shop, therefore I am!" advertised openly in a London store. The pleasure afforded is often short-lived: the shopping bag is emptied and the contents soon forgotten. And yet we try to ignore these thoughts and feelings, we find them too unsettling, too difficult and so we take refuge in more work, more shopping, more possessions, more parties, entertainment, television and radio: "Human kind can not bear very much reality." (T.S.Eliot)

Karl Marx saw religion as the opium of the people, but these days it is not religion but *consuming* that is our drug. Some of us prefer to be 'out of our mind' in one way or the other, rather than take advantage of our innate potential for growth and insight.

Beyond ego consciousness

The awareness of different levels of consciousness has been brought out by 20th century psychologists: "Our normal waking consciousness is but one special type of consciousness, while all about it, parted from it by the flimsiest of screens, there lie potential forms of consciousness entirely different." (William James, *Varieties of Religious Experience*)

Whereas Freud discovered the unconscious and treated it in mechanistic terms, Jung's work led him to the conviction that there were other aspects to the unconscious, and postulated even a higher consciousness. But he was very aware that this view went counter to the prevailing worldview: "The assumption that the human psyche possesses layers that lie below consciousness is not likely to arouse serious opposition. But that there could just as well be layers lying above consciousness seems to be a surmise which borders on high treason against human nature."

According to Jung, the matrix of the unconscious holds both the *personal unconscious* and the *collective unconscious,* which contains ancestral memories and the *archetypes,* patterns of cosmic energy, both destructive and creative. The *self* links there into the Spirit. It leads us first to descend to the depth of our personal unconscious, to all that is suppressed there both good and bad, so that it can be brought to awareness and healed. Then it helps us to rise creatively to the heights of the transpersonal consciousness in all wholeness. The same force that causes the sense of dissatisfaction is the one that enables the integration, the healing.

Just acknowledging the existence of these different levels of awareness seems to open the door to our transforming our consciousness, from restricting ourselves to a narrow, confining one – the ego – to including a wider all-embracing one – the *self.* It leads us to wholeness and fullness of life; then we discover that the essential centre of our being is one with the centre of all Being.

"The little space within the heart is as great as this vast universe. The heavens and the earth are there, and the sun, and the moon, and the stars; fire and lightening and winds are there; and all that now is and all that is not: for the whole universe is in Him and He dwells within our heart." (Chandogya Upanishad)

CHAPTER SIX

Purifying the emotions by watching the thoughts

In the previous chapters we have looked at how thoughts, both superficial and unconscious conditioned thoughts, can hinder us on the path of meditation and in our life. We have looked at ways of dealing with the surface ones; now we will look at ways of dealing with deeper 'survival' thoughts. We will look at a practice that can help us to become more self-aware of the hidden ways the behaviour of the ego is motivated.

We need effective ways of purifying the emotions, the 'soul'. Therefore ways of purifying thoughts and desires are found in many of the traditions, as we are dealing with a universal human problem. The Buddhists' discipline of 'watching the mind' leading to 'detachment' comes very close to the advice we find in the Christian tradition in the teachings of the Desert of the 4th century, in particular Evagrius Ponticus. His thought is a continuation of speculation on the role of the 'passions', the unpurified emotions of earlier centuries.

By purifying our emotions we will be able to reach our 'spirit', our self and come to a balanced harmonious state of being which is guided by compassion.

* * * * *

To become truly free and able to connect with the *self* we must break through the automatic responses caused by our '*unmet survival needs*' out of which our *ego* operates. We need to see reality unhindered by our emotional and psychological conditioning. We need to become aware of these motives, the needs underlying our actions and realise that they are often reactions out of time, relevant to the past but not to the present situation. This *purification* of the desires of the *ego* is considered an essential practice by all mystics. They would have all agreed with Blake when he said: "a fool sees not the same tree that a wise man sees."

Evagrius, one of the most important of the Desert Fathers gives very clear instructions in his books, *Praktikos* and *Chapters on Prayer*. His books are a collection of sayings, some very *koan* like. Their meaning is not obvious, often a summary of a particular train of thought. They need to be lived with and their meaning intuitively sensed. Thomas Merton in *Zen and the Birds of Appetite* calls him a Zen Master. Evagrius' life, upbringing and experience had given him not only a clear Christian theology but also perceptive insight into the working of the human mind. His own experience in the first part of his life as a successful speaker and socialite with its attendant temptations, followed by the rest of his life in solitude and silence in the Desert, gave him first hand experience of the difficulties on the spiritual path.

Evagrius' main teacher, Origen, explained in his theology that we were all at first one with the Divine. But for some reason that is not at all clear we turned away from this unity. Origen says we were 'sated', in other words, we were bored. Then God in his compassion made a new creation for us; we were given a body, our rational intelligence, a *soul,* the seat of the emotions, and an appropriate environment. But we retained still the *nous,* our Divine intuitive intelligence, our *spirit*/our *self.* This maintained our essential link with the Divine, enabling our potential return.

The *soul* is the enlivening principle that gives richness to life through emotional, psychological deepening of any experience. The *soul* and the *spirit* are integrally connected; moreover the *soul* is also the intermediary between the *ego* and the *self.* But the *soul,* as an intermediary, can both be a hindrance and a help. On the one hand it is an essential ingredient of being truly human and therefore the emotions cannot be discarded, but on the other hand if emotions are overwhelming and steered primarily by our *unmet* needs residing in the *shadow* they need to be purified. Otherwise the *soul* can cloud our perception of reality and obstruct access to the *self* and thus to Ultimate Reality. A purified *soul* becomes more and more identical with the *spirit.*

Demons

Evagrius was highly respected for his sound advice on how to cleanse the thoughts overlaid with strong emotions. We will see that when he talks about *passions, evil thoughts* and *demons (logismoi* in Greek) he is talking in Jungian terms about *archetypes* of thoughts residing in the *collective unconscious,* concept fields woven out of thought and emotion. These *archetypes* feed the *shadow* in the *personal unconscious:* in other words, our unpurified thoughts tap into these latent energies and are amplified by them. He was a man of his time, so we have to allow him naming these *demons.* But since they are very powerful it is not difficult to understand why these forces were given distinct entities.

The discussion of the *passions* started with the Greeks. Evagrius tapped into a rich vein of philosophical thought. The Stoics saw them as *disordered desires,* a *disease of the soul.* Aristotle, however, did not see the *passions* as either vices or virtues. To him they were neutral – it all depended on the use we make of them. And this is easy to see: if they are used, following blind urges, competitively to the detriment of others, they become a vice. If they are used in a *purified* form and in cooperation with others, to the benefit of all, they are virtues.

Plato agreed, and stressed that we need all the *passions.* He used the analogy of a charioteer driving a two-horse carriage. One of the horses is of noble blood, the other unruly and rebellious. To be able to move effectively we need both horses, well controlled and handled by the charioteer – the mind. To him the essence was to understand, accept and use all sides of our *passions* and bring them into harmony.

The Desert Fathers and Mothers varied enormously in their teachings.

The simple Coptic monks were like the Stoics and felt that *passions* were *disordered desires* and should be uprooted; others like Evagrius were closer to Plato and saw them as misdirected emotions, needing to be understood, controlled and purified.

The way these unconscious mental forces power our mind is shown, dressed in a different symbolic cultural guise, in the training of a lama in Tibet. The disciples spend months visualising and building up a *tulpa*, a mental construct, which often takes the shape of a fearful demon with seemingly a life of its own. More often than not the disciples are externalising their own inner *demons*. When this mental construct has become totally real to them and even seems to threaten them, they are instructed by their teacher to destroy it, as it is only a product of their thought and imagination. Not only does it test their fearlessness, but it demonstrates to the disciple the illusionary power of their own mind.

Evagrius clearly saw the effect these *demons* had on our ordinary thoughts. Something in our thoughts resonated with these *archetypal* energies and thus attracted them. And that is the crux. Thoughts in themselves are not bad. Only when we intend to *act* on thoughts driven by *passions, unmet needs,* do we allow the *demons* in. The *demons* he discusses are: *gluttony, then impurity, avarice, sadness, anger, acedia, vainglory,* and last but not least *pride.* The most important ones that drive us are *gluttony (greed)* and *pride*. All the other *thoughts* follow logically from these two.

Greed is seen as an *over*-indulgence in the senses in general, and so applies to food/drink, possessions and sex. That in turn leads to *avarice* – we want to keep what we have – or to *sadness* – we do not have everything we would like to. Then *anger* (and *envy*) arises towards those who have what we lack, or who try to take our possessions away from us. Then in turn come *vainglory* and *pride;* we want to show off our possessions and achievements and claim all the credit for them, and not accept them as the result of talents we have received as a gift from the Divine. *Impurity* is also seen in these terms. Love and sex should not be driven by *greed*, selfish over-indulgence. Love becomes *impurity* when it is not an expression of pure love but a means of exploiting or possessing the other for our own needs rather than respecting the true value of the other. Hence it does not necessarily mean abstinence – marriage was acceptable.

The link between Evagrius' *passions* and our *survival needs,* especially those that are perceived as *unmet,* is very clear. The normal ordinary acceptable need to have sufficient possessions for survival becomes an overwhelming drive i.e. *greed* for possession of things and people, which will give us the illusory sense of *love, pleasure, security, esteem, power and control* that we crave. Even at that time the link between survival and the *passions* was clearly seen: "The cause of this deviation of the natural energies into destructive passions is the hidden fear of death." (Maximus the Confessor, 7th century). Fear of death is the other side of the coin of survival drives. We may not consciously fear death, but we all have a healthy survival instinct.

✐ Through *greed* and *pride* the ego hijacks our whole being into self-centredness, *ego*-centredness. The *ego,* the survival instinct, by itself is essential. But what we have to avoid is the *demonic* dominance of the *ego* through our perceived or real *unmet needs.* Then we are not free, but literally *demonically* possessed.

Dealing with our *demons* can seem quite a task, as awareness increases at first the intensity of our emotional wounds. But real awareness, becoming conscious of the link between our drives and the consequent chain of reactions, is the only way to confront our *demons.* However painful it is, we do need to face and understand our patterns before we can rise above them and be freed from them. In a way they are our best teachers – we learn more from contemplating our weaknesses than our strengths. "Take away temptations and no one will be saved." (Evagrius)

Therefore we have to stay with this process despite everything; we have to carry on with our daily discipline, even if it is very tough: "Nothing is as difficult as not deceiving oneself". (Wittgenstein)

In addition to our usual meditation sessions, it is very useful at certain times to practice visualization techniques to help the process of not deceiving ourselves. Imaginative contemplation as recommended by St Ignatius of Loyola, which is very similar to Jungian imagination, is an excellent way of allowing material to rise from the unconscious to conscious leading to insight, when done with guidance in a controlled safe setting.

Evagrius, Freud, Jung and many other modern therapists consider insight *the* principle that will resolve conflicts emerging from the personal unconscious. As long as they are unconscious we have no control over these forces. By their becoming conscious through insight, by our acknowledging and accepting them, we rob them of their power and healing can start. Awareness is all important.

"Men are admitted into heaven not because they have curbed and governed their passions or have no passions, but because they have cultivated their understanding." (William Blake, *A Vision of the Last Judgment*)

Insights, awareness makes us conscious of the problems, but that does not necessarily mean we have the solutions. For that we need the critical faculties of our rational mind, Plato's *charioteer*, with its objectivity, detachment and awareness guided by intuition to clarify this insight.

To come to awareness it is helpful to introduce a gap. Just as we become aware of the gaps in our breathing and between the thoughts, we insert a gap between intention of action and the actual action.

Watching the thoughts

According to Evagrius the way to identify our personal *demons* is twofold: by *prayer/meditation* – by calling on spiritual powers to help us – and by *effort* to come to self-knowledge and awareness, which is achieved by *watching the thoughts.* Evagrius is not asking us to watch the usual trivial junk that floats over the surface of our mind. That would be pointless and excruciatingly boring. He is concerned about the deep thoughts that are either expressions of our unmet needs and unpurified desires or desires coming from our deeper spiritual nature. We need to pay these significant thoughts and their associations the attention they deserve. They are the only indicators we have of what really motivates us for good or for ill.

The first stage is identification. We need to listen carefully to the program on our own internal radio. What are the persistent, recurring thoughts? Sift the trivial from the more significant ones by labelling them. What is the desire feeding this?

Watching the thoughts, watching the mind is an activity done in Buddhist practices during the period of meditation. But it soon becomes clear that what Evagrius is recommending is an awareness of thoughts, emotions and actions outside the actual prayer/meditation periods: watching the thoughts as they float into our awareness at any time and really understand what is the desire or need that drives them.

The sequence leading to thoughts and actions

Evagrius is in fact outlining the process of the unfolding of memories through the various stages, which amplify desires and the resulting action. We need to work backwards and start with our thoughts, becoming aware of the connections and associations between them. Then we need to take one step back to the feeling that caused the thought. Feelings are thoughts felt in our body before we give shape to their meaning.

The problem is that we are conditioned to ignore our feelings because of their seemingly irrational nature. They are, however, the first indication that we have that there is something stirring in our unconscious depth. We need therefore to become aware and acknowledge our feelings rather than suppress them. As soon as we become conscious of a feeling we should ask ourselves, where this is coming from, what really is the issue at hand, what conditioned memories are being tapped into?

Before we become conscious of a feeling there often has been according to Evagrius a sensation of some sort: a sound, the way the light falls and especially a taste or smell. But underpinning these sensations and feelings is an archetypal image coming from the *demon* at work in our *personal and collective unconscious.* These images reside primarily in the right brain, as we shall see. Recognizing this image helps us to obtain insight into our motivations and our basic desires, which are calling for expression.

The most striking example of a sense impression being the cause of first *feeling* and then *thought* occurs in the first book *Combray* of Proust's master piece, *A la Recherche du Temps perdu* (*Remembrances of Things Past*). He comes home one afternoon tired, depressed and dips a biscuit, a *petite madeleine* into his tea. The moment he tastes it, an intense feeling of joy flows through his entire being. Then he is overwhelmed by thoughts of his childhood.

This then is the inevitable chain of events as proposed by Evagrius: archetypal images, then sense impressions that invoke feelings, conditioned or free; these feelings lead in turn to thoughts, then to desires both positive and negative. Once we have reached this stage we seem to be programmed to automatically translate our strong desires into actions.

It is important to stress once more that the *demons* can gain influence on our life only through our thoughts. We need therefore to stop the above sequence before conditioned memory and imagination turn them into *disordered desires* and inevitably into action.

Meditation is the time when we temporarily silence the surface mind. Sometimes, though, a clear thought does arise during this period, which is very valuable. Insights do happen, as the meditative state allows information to pass from the unconscious to the conscious, from the *self* to the *ego*. And our unconscious picks up a lot more important background information than our conscious mind, when we are dealing with problems or issues in daily life. We need to reflect on these intuitive insights in the time away from meditation.

We need to be aware that our internal emotional state triggered by sense impressions, dreams, fears and fantasies will be reflected in the external circumstances we create. In Proust's case the strong feeling of nostalgia produced a work of art; sadly this is not the case for most of us.

The first line of defence, however, is avoiding the situations where we know by now that some of our *demons* are very strong due to our habitual responses over the years, making us translate some of our thoughts and emotions mindlessly into *knee-jerk* actions. It is therefore advisable to practice with the weaker *demons*. Change can only happen gradually, sometimes even imperceptibly. We need to take one small step at the time. We must not forget that it is not something we achieve solely by dint of our own effort. Our higher *self* links us to the Higher Spiritual Reality. Insights, inspiration and healing come from that Source. This input of our higher mind is indispensable for true insight and growth. All we need to do is clear our mind of surface clutter and be open.

Not only our thoughts but also our dreams are a way for Higher Reality to communicate with us. Jung considered dreams as messages from the unconscious. Ancient traditions considered dreams to be very important messages from the Divine – the Egyptian, Greek, Roman, Jewish and early Christian culture from Origen to St Augustine. All believed that dreams were part of the same spiritual reality that is accessed by prayer/meditation.

Not all dreams are important. Many of them are attempts of our mind to try to make sense of disconnected facts and experiences. In fact it is a way of clearing all the junk that clutters our subconscious. Significant dreams are often quite recognisably different. Clarity and lucidity seem to be the characteristics of messages from the Source.

Resistance to awareness and growth

Coming to awareness can be quite painful. Therefore the *ego* again throws up resistance, making us feel bored, tired and restless: Evagrius, like all the Desert Fathers, called this the *demon of acedia*. Rather than identifying this restlessness, boredom or other emotions as coming from the internal struggle or our own nature, we try to find reasons in things outside ourselves. We tend to project this feeling of dissatisfaction out and blame others for what we did or did not do: *It is the fault of our community, our parents, our society ...*

We try to justify the way we feel and behave with excuses, which seem plausible to us:

"A brother was restless in the community and often moved to anger. So he said: 'I will go and live somewhere by myself. And since I shall be able to talk or listen to no one, I shall be tranquil, and my passionate anger will cease.' He went out and lived alone in a cave. But one day he filled his jug with water and put it on the ground. It happened suddenly to fall over. He filled it again, and again it fell. And this happened a third time. And in a rage he snatched up the jug and broke it. Returning to his right mind, he knew that the demon of anger had mocked him, and he said: 'I will

127

return to the community. Wherever you live, you need effort and patience and above all God's help.' "

Blaming others can lead to us seeing ourselves moreover as a victim, which imprisons us and robs us of the freedom of our true humanity.

Our tendency to gossip about, judge and criticize others is another way we show our own unresolved conflicts: a clear sign that we have not yet *purified* our emotions. It links us with our conditioning, *unmet needs* and the resulting desires. We judge and criticize others for the behaviour potentially our own. "Never point a finger of scorn or judgment at your fellow man because when you point, there are three fingers pointing back at you." (Bear Heart, *The Wind is my Mother*)

But not only is it detrimental to us, but in judging we also take a freeze-frame of others, not allowing for their possible progress and growth. We deny them the possibility of change and trap them in a particular moment in time. "Abba Xanthias said, 'The thief was on the cross and he was justified by a single word; and Judas who was counted among the number of the apostles lost all his labour in one single night and descended from heaven to hell.'" (Stories from the Desert Fathers)

This *watching our thoughts,* helped by meditation, not only transforms our consciousness but also our life. The gifts of meditation become part of who we are and help to make our reaction to life's challenges more composed and balanced. With the benefit of this discipline we are gradually able to see ordinary reality unhindered by emotional burdens, conditioning and the survival drive. We reach "purity of heart ... a total acceptance of ourselves and of our situation ... renunciation of all deluded images of ourselves – all exaggerated estimates of our own capacities – in order to obey God's will as it comes to us." (Thomas Merton).

This *purity of heart*, which Evagrius called *apatheia*, does not mean being apathetic, being emotionless, but being *detached*. It is a state in which we are not driven, not overwhelmed by our emotions. Then everything we do is a pure act, appropriate to the needs of a given situation and unadulterated by any personal expectations or hidden agendas. Our actions become an expression of unselfish love – *agape*. The state of *apatheia* and *agape* are inseparably connected. "No one who loves true prayer and yet gives way to anger or resentment can be absolved from the imputation of madness. He resembles a man who wished to see clearly and for this purpose he scratched his eye." (Evagrius)

Thus we react to and transform our reality, our circumstances, with freedom and dignity. This in turn will allow us to relate to others with the same freedom. We will then experience our true *self* in the Divine through a pure *soul* without hindrances.

This true state of serenity, love, balance and harmony can only be reached by persevering. The stronger the demon of *acedia*, the closer we are to breaking through to this "deep peace and irrepressible joy." (Evagrius)

Evagrius stressed that we will know when we have reached that stage, "when the spirit begins to see its own light," an important thought in his time: *God is Light* and the *self* was the *Mirror of God*. Again we find this in other traditions as well. In the Hindu tradition we are told that we will experience the *inner light* of the Atman.

Spiritual friendship

In order to be able to act so *purely,* we see that we need to be aware of what hinders us. But we are not alone in this endeavour: the Divine within us guides and heals us by releasing the memories and their associated wounds gradually over time – purely by bringing them to our awareness.

But sometimes the Divine within can only help us with outside help to facilitate this process:

"How great are the needs of your creatures on this earth, O God. They sit there, talking quietly and quite unsuspecting, and suddenly their need erupts in all its nakedness. Then, there they are, bundles of human misery, desperate and unable to face life. And that's when my task begins.

One must ... clear the path towards you in them, God, and to do that one must be a keen judge of the human soul ... I embark on a slow voyage of exploration with everyone who comes to me ... And I thank you for the gift to be able to read people." (Etty Hillesum, *An Interrupted Life)*

Telling our story, telling our truth, in a journal, to a therapist or to a good friend, helps awareness and has a healing effect. Often the result of this is that the suppressed, rejected part of us gets accepted and thus integrated in the whole of our being.

Awareness is the key. Being *awake* in life, leads to realising our full potential and remembering our true nature:

"But you are home, cries the witch of the North. All you have to do is wake up!" (The Wizard of Oz)

CHAPTER SEVEN
The spectrum of consciousness

We have looked at the interaction between the ego and the self, but we need to see this interplay in a wider context. There is a distinct process of gradual evolution not only operating on a physical level but also in consciousness itself from our beginnings to the present and future time. We can see many of these stages mirrored clearly in the growth of awareness of a child. We also recognise similar developments on the societal and cultural level. Whereas people may be at different stages, the emphasis needs always to be on integration rather than suppression of the earlier stage. Furthermore, to reach the next stage in our human potential we have to integrate scientific perception of reality and 'mystical' perception of reality, in truth the ego and the self.

* * * * *

Scientists have proved that the right hemisphere of the brain is the oldest; this is the non-verbal, largely *unconscious* part of the brain, which functions in images and emotions, giving a holistic impression of the situation. The emotional component comes through the connections to the older limbic part of the brain.

The left-brain areas with their verbal and linear time orientation are the most recent ones, forming the *conscious* mind. The human consciousness is originally therefore at one with the wider all encompassing *unconscious* mind. On this matrix the *ego* circuit is then traced out. The *conscious* mind therefore develops out of the *unconscious*. The implication of this is that we can return to the original wider consciousness if we temporarily switch off the *ego* circuit – in fact, in Jesus' words when we "leave self behind." (Lk 9:23) Then we will become consciously aware of what at first was an unconscious state, interconnectedness with the Divine ground of our being. We return to our "original face before our parents were born." (Buddhist saying)

Just as our physical evolution has left traces in our bodies and is seen in the development of the embryo, the evolution of human consciousness in humankind in general can again be seen in our mental, psychological and emotional development from baby, to infant, to child, to adolescent and then to adult and finally to a fully actualised human person.[1]

In the evolution of consciousness as mirrored in a child's development, we start therefore with the *right-brain* activity of the *unconscious* mind. Apparently, when they are in the womb and in the early months after birth, babies sense no separation. They are still in their wider unity consciousness. They feel at one,

---

[1] See also Ken Wilber, *Up from Eden*, and Bede Griffiths, *A New Vision of Reality*.

first peacefully swimming in the amniotic fluid and then feeding at the breast. The mother is an extension of themselves, a puzzling one that may appear and disappear at intervals, but nevertheless is perceived as part of their own being. This is undifferentiated bliss. No sense of separation, no conscious sense of *ego* as yet. However, unconsciously the survival instinct is already at work.

Soon they become aware of a distinction between their own being, others and the environment. There is a growing awareness that the extension of themselves seems to differ at times. The baby starts to recognise different faces, is perhaps a bit concerned at this development and starts to respond with smiles – a sweet survival instinct that works a treat. Still the feeling is primarily one of unity. Consciousness at this stage is confined to the physical, sensual and emotional. There is no sense of linear time – they want to be fed when they are hungry – and no sense of space. This can be seen from observing difficulties with spatial coordination. These important qualities of the *ego* have not yet developed. Yet there is a growing sense of control. Experience teaches them when they cry that a face will appear. When they reach out they can touch something and make it move. Finally by six months, a sense of being separate is clearly there.

Over the next 18 months we see signs of a developing *ego:* verbal skills and a sense of time and space are developing. Moreover the *ego's* need to control the environment has become stronger. We enter the phase of *the terrible two's*: tantrums galore when their own will is thwarted. But simultaneously the awareness develops that other people have intentions and emotions too, separate from themselves, which may well conflict with the way they are feeling at the time. They are happy to be eating earth and are surprised when confronted by an annoyed anxious mother who stops it. We encourage children at this stage to play with other children; it teaches them to share and take the feelings of others into consideration. In doing so, we reinforce at the same time their need to be accepted by others. Acceptance becomes important at that stage: by the age of three we see them modifying their *ego* already to fit in. They will give in when they sense that the other child is getting unhappy and are able to wait to take turns.

At this early stage from two years on, thinking is still based on *right brain* activity: "EEG studies of the brain of children under five show that they permanently function in alpha mode – the state of altered consciousness in an adult – rather than the beta mode of ordinary mature consciousness." (Lynne Taggart, *The Field*)

Qualities such as intuition, imagination and feelings, linked with the *self*, are foremost. The dividing line between reality and fantasy is not very clear. Dreams and fantasies are acted out in everyday life. Children would agree with the statement: "I do not know whether I was a man dreaming I was a butterfly, or whether I am now a butterfly dreaming I was a man." (Chuang Tzu, *On Leveling all Things*) Fears, which seem unreasonable to the adult, are real.

The child is therefore still in touch with the contents of the wider consciousness, the *archetypes* from our *collective unconscious*. The child is surrounded by different entities: fairies, aliens. Fairies *do* live at the bottom of the garden or in the trees. Aliens *do* come, talk and make you laugh.

Trees, flowers, the moon and the stars are alive and fascinating. The inner and outer realities interpenetrate and are magically connected.

Psychic powers we possibly all possessed at an earlier stage of human development are still operational at this stage because the connection between the *self* and the rest of creation has not yet been severed. Prescience, telepathy is not uncommon. Children know instinctively, when something is wrong with someone they love and often catch a person's intention long before an adult does.

Time is cyclical at this stage, judged by the sun, the moon and the seasons. This same understanding of time we still find in Native American culture and with the world's most ancient people, the Aborigines of Australia, who distinguish linear time from *Dream Time*, cyclical and yet co-existing: the time of myths and ancestors linked with the Now.

There is also a feeling of omnipotence and a conviction of the power of thought. If something is wished for in anger and then *does* happen, for instance, if a parent dies in an accident after the child had violent thoughts against this parent, there is a terrible sense of guilt and a feeling of responsibility. They really feel they have caused this death. Since these feelings are hardly ever shared or confided to an adult, the burden of 'wish-fulfilment' can have a quite traumatic effect on the child.

The *definite* switch over from right brain activity to left brain activity starts around school age, when the child is 5 or 6 years old. Writing and reading encourages logical thought, a left-brain activity. Qualities associated with left-brain activity – logic, assertiveness, aggression, competition – are further strengthened by competitive exams. Time becomes linear; a sense of history develops. The matrix of the *ego* is now clearly put in place. *Right brain activity* – intuition, imagination, and feeling connected to everyone, caring – is not always valued by society and the peer group, in fact often ridiculed, hence repressed. The emphasis at this stage of the development is on conforming to the rules and regulations that dominate a particular culture. Children want to be accepted and have strong *survival instincts*, and will suppress those parts of their behaviour or consciousness that are frowned on. Awareness of the wider community is very strong at this age; the feeling of not being part of the *gang* can be quite devastating.

From the early teenage years onwards, the *ego* dominance urges the individual to move away from community and make their own mark separately. But it is also possible that with the drive to strike out on their own, they come in touch with other viewpoints and cultures. Rules, regulations and long held beliefs may then be questioned. Often at this state they outgrow the inherited image of God and begin looking at these conditioned images and searching for an image that resonates with them. In fact they are slowly liberating themselves from the *survival* dominance of the *ego* and may well become aware of the *self* calling them home to unity consciousness.

Stages of cultural development

This is a simplified view of child development, but it does show how growth goes hand in hand with coping strategies dictated by the rise of the *ego*. Development of the individual is a mirror image of the stages of humanity's cultural development, as outlined by Ken Wilber in his book, *Up from Eden.*

At first the individual does not feel any sense of separation either from the tribe or the environment. Behaviour is intuitive, instinctive with feeling and sense impressions dominating. Slowly awareness of a separate identity emerges, but still the connection with the natural world is magical. There is a strong, psychic identification with particular animals seen as *spirit guides* or *totems* – we still get an insight into this stage in the Native American and Aboriginal cultures. Then with the development of settled communities, the strong emphasis on community is maintained but the sense of the separate *ego* becomes stronger. Finally individuals see themselves as standing apart from both the community and nature.

This is the evolutionary stage our Western culture has reached on the whole, which is shown in what we consider admirable qualities: assertiveness, strong sense of competition, ruthlessness to achieve power and position – all ego qualities. The *ego* is fully developed and assertive and qualities of the *self* are suppressed, such as love of justice, truth and goodness.

However, we must not forget that this development is not uniform. At each stage there are individuals who outstrip their fellow human beings, as can be seen by the shamans of earlier cultures and the mystics of all traditions and ages. How many times have we heard that someone's thought is *beyond their time*? But there are also those who lag behind as seen in the regression that is fundamentalism.

The next step forward is integration of the perceived polarity between the two sides of our being into a harmonic whole by being aware of and balancing these different qualities, intuition and reason, *the ego* and the *self*; in doing so we reactivate the connections between both sides of the brain. This is the next natural stage of our development; the potentiality for it exists in us all. The choice and challenge we face is to stay in the *ego* stage and possibly destroy ourselves or transcend to the next stage of evolution by integrating the totality of our being. The reward is the *conscious* sense of unity with everyone, nature and the Divine that we experienced *unconsciously* at our beginning.

Repression rather than integration

The emphasis in this development of consciousness should be on integration. Each previous stage needs to be consciously understood and then assimilated in the next stage. If this does not happen and we repress the earlier stages, an imbalance arises. Unfortunately, as we have seen, this is more often than not what we do – we separate out, repress rather than include. Thus we arrest our emotional development.

Fear can drive us back to earlier developmental stages: we cling to the mother at the school gate, and we curl up in a fetal position when badly hurt, even as an adult. Fear can also keep us at a developmental stage when we felt secure and happy. The *Peter Pan* syndrome and *Walter Mitty* behaviour are both symptoms of this type of arrested development.

Unhappy events can keep us at an earlier stage. Often in a grown-up person we can see the child at the age when he/she was traumatically hurt. The experience has not been understood and integrated but repressed; yet it can at times come to the fore, showing itself in behaviour appropriate only to an earlier developmental stage. An example of this is a person who was badly hurt at age six, when she was sent to be with an aunt for a year. When she came back home there was a new baby. She felt betrayed and rejected by her mother. Often under stress her reactions are those of a six year old: emotional tantrums and a total overreaction, perfectly acceptable from a young child but not from one of her age.

Scientific consciousness

The emphasis of humanity in the developed West is at present on the rational mind experiencing the material world, the world of the senses: we are scientists collecting data. We are pattern-seeking creatures by nature: neuroscience reveals we seek patterns even when there are none, as some of our dreams show. This is our way of making sense of what we perceive on the intellectual level. It can lead to a conviction that all can be understood at this rational level even the Divine:

"However, if we do discover a complete theory, it should in time be understandable in broad principle by everyone, not just a few scientists. Then we shall all, philosophers, scientists, and just ordinary people, be able to take part in the discussion of the question of why it is that we and the universe exist. If we find the answer to that, it would be the ultimate triumph of human reason – for then we would know the mind of God." (Stephen Hawking, *A Brief History of Time*)

Material scientists like Stephen Hawking and Richard Dawkins are of the opinion that everything arises from matter including consciousness. They see the brain as the origin of consciousness, which could easily be compared to saying that the radio itself produces the music. Other scientists like David Bohm consider the Ultimate Reality as the source of both energy and consciousness; matter unfolds from it and manifests it. The brain is the instrument of receiving and interpreting the Cosmic Consciousness.

Different levels of knowing

The experiences of the mystics tend to agree with the second explanation. They stress that different ways of knowing are needed at different levels of consciousness. In fact, on the spiritual path we need to retrace our steps from the *ego* level to the *self*.

On the material plane we perceive with our ordinary eyes, the *Eye of the Flesh*. This is the *ego* level characterised by duality, by the division between *subject* and *object*. We constantly distinguish ourselves as separate, create boundaries and impose patterns. It is the level of our surface thoughts, images and feelings: "chaotic din of a mind ravaged by so much exposure to trivia and distraction." (John Main) and here "we meet the ego in its most frazzled state, dressed in the ever-changing costumes of daily life." (Laurence Freeman).

Once we manage to quieten the mind, we leave the outside world, but are still on the *ego* level. We enter a deeper level, the level of buried feelings and memories, our *personal unconscious*. There we see with the *Eye of the Mind* and colour the outside reality with our thoughts, emotions and feelings, and create the landscape of our mind. The *ego* is here "dressed in the more dramatic period costumes of the different stages of our psychological history, acting out its many roles." (Laurence Freeman)

When we manage to acknowledge and accept what comes up, we arrive at a deeper level, the level of the *self*. We now perceive intuitively with the *Eye of the Heart*. First we become aware of the *collective unconscious*, where we touch the universal symbols/archetypes, timeless psychic forces.

Then finally we reach beyond and transcend to the level of the Spiritual Reality that is the Source of all. This is the level of integration where object and subject once more become one: *The Knower, the Knowing and the Known are one.* This is "the level of silence, where we see with wonder the light of our own spirit and where we contact the ground of our being." (John Main) At this level "we confront the ego in its naked existence, all the costumes temporarily laid aside." (Laurence Freeman).

At this level we still sense things but without use of the ordinary sense organs and unrelated to the environment in which we find ourselves. Origen (3rd Century) was the first Christian teacher to speak about *the spiritual senses.* It is a way of perceiving that is quite different from the physical, this perception with the *spiritual senses.* We see with our eyes closed; we hear in the silence. Visual and auditory manifestations are perceived directly without intermediaries. Furthermore, when we become more intimately aware of the Divine there is even a different sense of tasting, smelling and touching. "I shall give you what no eye has seen, what no ear has heard, what no hand has touched, what has nor arisen in the human heart." (Gospel of Thomas 17)

But we also then become painfully aware that by being on this material plane we are separated from Ultimate Reality. This is the last hurdle the *ego* has to overcome. It has to let go of its sense of an isolated finite existence and accept that this too is a construct of our mind. Only then can we find our true Self in union with the All. This is seen as the ultimate aim of life on earth, this return to union with the Divine: "The whole purpose of this life is to restore to health the eye of the heart by which God may be seen." (St Augustine)

These three levels are aspects of our consciousness, which unfold with time, deepening and overlapping. In meditation we keep touching these various levels at different stages of our journey in a spiral fashion. Touching the deepest level may well be the start of our spiritual journey, as we have seen. We keep learning and growing. More of our barriers dissolve as emotional wounds are understood and thus healed, allowing us to accept the *shadow*. Slowly we are able to detach from our conditioning and our need to use the world and other people as emotional props for survival. The more we enter the silence and stillness of meditation, the more we recover our intuitive understanding and begin to integrate this with our rational consciousness. By allowing each to inform the other we bring together the mind and the heart in balance and harmony. We have then integrated all our facets, *ego* and *self* and have reached our full human potential.

One Zen meditator asks another: *"What happens next?" The other replies, "What do you mean, what happens next, this is it!"*

CHAPTER EIGHT

The Ultimate Reality

In this chapter we will be looking at what this 'it' is, although this Ultimate Reality is unknowable and incomprehensible to our rational intelligence. We have seen in the 'Perennial Philosophy' that there is in all traditions the belief that we can experience the essence of this reality, as there is something within the human being that is similar to it. To help us on the path towards this experience there is a clear map. Nature is both seen as a means to experiencing this other Reality and also as a way of manifesting and making visible the Ultimate Invisible. At this level abstract concepts are used to approximate this Reality. The essential attitude needed on this journey is one of staying fearlessly in the present moment.

* * * * *

The complementarity and essential balance of the two sides of our nature is beautifully captured in the symbol of the *Tao*. *Yin* is the *earth – matter –* and the *feminine* aspect and *Yang* is the *heaven* – *spirit* – and the *masculine* aspect of creation. In the course of this book the *ego* has been linked in contrast with *matter*, the *masculine* and the left side of the brain and the *self* with the *feminine*, the *spirit* and the right side of the brain. This cross-over beautifully brings out the basic equality of both the aspects of creation. Each is equally important and in total balance with each other; each contains the seed of the other in this philosophy. The human being is considered to be the important link, the bridge between the two.

We need to give equal importance to these different aspects in ourselves; our practice helps us to activate the neural connections between the right and left side of the brain bringing about balance and harmony.

We see the same emphasis of integration and transformation in the *Gospel of Thomas*:

"Jesus said to them, 'When you make the two into one, and when you make the inner like the outer and the outer like the inner, and the upper like the lower, and when you make male and female into a single one..... then you will enter the kingdom." (Saying 22)

Making the two into one, the material and the spiritual,

bringing together the *ego* and the *self*, has been the inspiration and the underlying *leitmotiv* of this book. We need to let our true divine nature at our core, the *self*, permeate the whole of our outer being, the *ego*, so that our behaviour is guided by both. Thus we divinise our whole being, by opening *the lower*, the material, to the Spirit, the Light, *the higher*.

The needed integration of all aspects of our being, including *male* and *female*, is highlighted in a way Jung would have approved of: the integration of the *animus* and the *anima*. Then we will *enter the kingdom*, experience the *being* and *presence* of the Divine.

Union with the Divine

The early Church fathers had no shadow of a doubt that union with the Divine is possible for all: "God is the life of all free beings. He is the salvation of all, of believers and unbelievers, of the just or the unjust, of the pious or the impious, of those freed from passions or those caught up in them, of monks or those living in the world, of the educated and the illiterate, of the healthy and the sick, of the young and the old. He is like the outpouring of light, the glimpse of the sun, or the changes of the weather which are the same for everyone." (Gregory of Nyssa)

The reason for this is to be found in their theology. The Greek philosophers, in particular Plato, were the first to formulate the idea of our having something essential in common with the Divine. They called it the *nous*, pure intuitive intelligence as distinct from rational intelligence. Having something like the

Divine within us allows us to know the Divine, as the prevalent idea in early thought was that only *like can know like*. Our everyday experience also confirms that. We know that for communion to be possible there has to be likeness; only when we have something substantial in common with another person can we truly relate to them, can we be one in mind and soul.

The early Church Father, Clement of Alexandria, saw the correspondence between the concept of *nous* and the one expressed in *Genesis* of being created in the *image of God*. Following him Origen, the Cappadocian Fathers, Evagrius and even later Meister Eckhart all saw this *image of God* as eternal and originally one with God.

It is best described by Origen in his cosmology. In the beginning we were one with the Divine solely as *pure intuitive consciousnesses*, the highest possible level of awareness. Then a choice was made to leave this pure state of being, described as an act of disobedience towards God. Origen called it being *sated* or *negligent*. In his theology the only one not to do this was the pure consciousness of Christ who stayed in union.

By choosing to turn away from the Divine state we became incarnate. We made a free choice with its inevitable consequence; we fell from this high level of consciousness to a lower one. This movement between levels of consciousness is imaged as the *fall* in Christianity. Yet we were given by the Divine all we needed, a body, a soul – the seat of emotions – and the appropriate environment. But in the highest part of the soul we retained our original link with the Divine, the *nous,* our spirit.

Neither Origen nor Meister Eckhart saw being created as a punishment, but as an educative act of Divine mercy. The essence of life is therefore to learn the truths of our existence and in doing so grow and work our way back to God, to *come home.* For this reason we were not only given the *nous,* our Divine beacon guiding us home but also the *survival needs* we needed on this material plane.

In moving towards this denser level of reality and consciousness we forgot, however, who we truly were. As is stated in the *Gospel of Thomas,* we are *all drunk*; we are *blind in our hearts.* After time, once we allow *our guardian angel,* our *self,* to remind us of our essential nature, we are able to make the journey *home* by focusing on the *spark* of our original consciousness. The return to union is therefore a free choice available to everyone.

Perhaps the real meaning of *original sin* is to turn our back on our spiritual origin and become attached and confined to the material *ego* level and its *survival needs.* St Paul too appears to describe *sin* in these terms: "Those who live on the level of our lower nature have their outlook formed by it, and that spells death; but those who live on the level of the spirit have the spiritual outlook, and that is life and peace." We have often understood this in a literal way as referring to sex. But it could also be taken to mean that a distinction is drawn between different levels of consciousness. We can understand *lower nature* perhaps more as the drives of the *ego,* and interpret the contrast he draws as the one between the attraction of the *ego* and the *self.*

The reason why we can touch and be touched therefore by this ultimate transpersonal reality is because there is something within us that is similar to this reality. Jung too was convinced that we can experience that reality, the source of both physical and mental forms, the *unus mundus.* In his view we encompass this underlying unifying structure from birth.

In all Wisdom traditions it is stressed that this essential part of human beings – whichever words we use for it – is the common ground between us and the Divine. We are talking about "that universal consciousness in which all living beings partake in the centre of their being and to which humankind may gain access, if we are ready to forget our little ego." (Lama Govinda)

The concept of a *universal consciousness* was first given the term *logos* by the Greeks philosophers, starting with Heraclites (5th century BC). God was the guiding force: "in the midst of all flux and opposites there is one-ness." Laurence Freeman defined the *logos* as "mind, power and purpose … the inner coherence and identity within all, the interconnecting quality in all things."

Later this concept changed slightly and the *logos* became the bridge between the Creator and creation. In the *Gospel of John* it was Christ who embodied the *Logos,* the Word, and was this bridge. Through our *nous,* our intuitive intelligence, we are able to connect with the *logos,* with this bridge.

We hear about this indwelling of the Divine Energy in the

Gospel of Thomas: "Jesus said, 'If your leaders say to you, look, *the kingdom is in heaven*, then the birds of heaven will precede you. If they say to you, *it is in the sea*, then the fish will precede you. Rather, the Kingdom is inside you and it is outside you.'" By *Kingdom* is meant the *Presence* of God, the Divine Energy.

Meditation helps us to actually experience this living force as Christ within us, energising, healing, transforming and leading us to greater awareness, wholeness and compassion.

Union with the Divine in other Wisdom traditions

In the Hindu philosophy the *Atman*, the eternal *self*, is one with *Brahman*, the cosmic divine Presence. The Sanskrit statement *tat tvam asi* ("thou art that") encapsulates this beautifully, as expressed in the *Chandogya Upanishads* as follows:

Svetaketu, who has returned home after, having learnt the Vedas, is very proud of his learning and has a great opinion of himself. His father asks him:

"Have you asked for that knowledge whereby what is not heard is heard, what is not thought is thought, and what is not known is known?"

"What is that knowledge, father?" asked Svetaketu.

"Bring me a fruit from the banyan tree."

"Here it is, father."

"Break it."

"It is broken, Sir."

"What do you see in it?"

"Very small seeds, Sir."

"Break one of them, my son."

"It is broken, Sir."

"What do you see in it?"

"Nothing at all, Sir."

Then the father spoke to him: "My son, from the very essence in the seed, which you cannot see, comes in truth this vast Banyan tree. Believe me, my son, an invisible and subtle essence is the Spirit of the whole universe. That is Reality. That is Atman. Thou art That."

This of course does not mean that *I* in my *ego* aspect and God are one: we are talking about an aspect of God and the deeper *self*. God is not confined to dwelling in our heart but is both immanent and transcendent.

Whereas in Buddhism there is no belief in a Creator God, yet there is the thought that we all possess the *Buddha nature*, which can merge with the *Dharmakaya*. When the Buddha stressed that we are *non-Atman* he was referring to the *ego*. He was a practical person, just like Jesus, and following in his footsteps Evagrius and the Desert Fathers, concerned with making us aware of the limitations of the personal *ego* and how to escape the influence of its *unmet needs*.

This view of identity between something in our soul and the Divine we find also expressed in a Sufi saying: "I saw my Lord with my heart's eye and said: 'Who art Thou, Lord?' 'Thyself', He replied." Immanuel Kant's *transcendental ego* is an attempt of philosophy *to express* this commonality with the Divine.

In drawing correspondences between different religions and philosophies in this way we must be careful not to deny the Truth each age discovers for itself: "in the image of Christ we are not just recycling a myth, but the particular actualisation of something cosmic and universal." (Laurence Freeman) We build on thought that has preceded us, but we still express in a unique way our perception of the Divine Ground and our relationship to it.

Similarity or identity

Similarity has always been accepted within Christianity – the soul as a mirror of God – but total identity has often been disputed. Yet we hear in the *Gospel of Thomas:* "Whoever drinks from my mouth will become like me; I myself shall become that person, and the hidden things will be revealed to that person." In the *Gospel of John* we find the same idea expressed: "that they may be one, even as we are one: I in them, and thou in me that they may be made perfect in one."

When we remember our true identity we *know* and *see* on an intuitive level, then we see *eye to eye:* "The eye in which I see God is the same eye in which God sees me. My eye and God's eye are one eye and one seeing, one knowing and one loving." (Meister Eckhart)

Constantly, mystics who experienced this identity and spoke about it were viewed with suspicion. Meister Eckhart talked about the birth of the *Word* in the soul: "Similarly I have often said that there is something in the soul that is closely related to God that it is one with him and not just united." Meister Eckhart in his *Sister Catherine Treatise* has Catherine say to her confessor: "Father, rejoice with me, I have become God." Often mystics talk about this state of permanent union, this total oneness. St Teresa of Avila talked in the *Interior Castle* about the seventh dwelling place of the spiritual marriage as a permanent state of union beyond rapture.

Yet it is communion rather than union we are talking about. It is not seen in Christianity as a total merging, but "there is no doubt that the individual loses all sense of separation from the One and experiences a total unity, but that does not mean that the individual no longer exists. Just as every element in nature is a unique reflection of the one Reality, so every human being is a unique centre of consciousness in the universal consciousness." (Bede Griffiths, *The Marriage of East and West*)

The Divine

Only in spiritual *experience* is real knowledge of this Ultimate Reality communicated at a deep level. The mystics of all ages and cultures have pointed out the difficulty in conveying their transpersonal experiences. The only medium we have to express our thoughts in – apart from images – is language. Modern philosophers have also amply demonstrated how unreliable and limited this mode of expression is. We are trying to describe the indescribable:

> *The tao that can be told*
> *is not the eternal Tao.*
> *The name that can be named*
> *is not the eternal Name.*

Words cannot begin to encompass the Divine. When we try to do it, there is the danger of words becoming idols; perhaps that is the reason Jesus did not write anything down himself. He used parables to illustrate the meaning of the reality he pointed to.

Clement of Alexandria (2nd century) was the first Christian Church Father to express the thought that God was beyond our understanding:

"God is beyond the One. He is ineffable, beyond all speech, beyond every concept, beyond every thought ... God is not in space, but above both place and time and name and thought. God is without limits, without form, without name."

Stages of experience

Although the Divine cannot be grasped by our ordinary intelligence, our stages of experiential perception of the Divine can be described. Origen's map of Christian growth (3rd C) points to three levels of development on the spiritual path, which will make the experience of the Divine Presence a reality.

The first development is the one we have been concentrating on: *practice, purifying the emotions,* thus clarifying our vision.

The second stage of development is sensing the Presence of the Divine through the contemplation of nature: "As for those who are far from God ... God made it possible for them to come near to the knowledge of him and his love for him through the medium of creatures." (Evagrius)

Our experience here is essentially one of the *presence* of the Divine rather than *union* with it. The main response is one of self-forgetting awe and wonder: "Only wonder can comprehend his incomprehensible power." (Gregory of Nissa) We saw an example of that in the first *awakening* experience of Bede Griffiths.

This is the level everyone can reach. We become aware of the Divine essence in everyone and everything; we are very conscious at this stage of our inter-connectedness. Yet we are still in the world and very much a part of it. It is the level of the *contemplative in action*, who acts from his/her spiritual centre and therefore out of compassion. There is a very good illustration of this attitude in a story about St Antony:

St Antony had prayed to the Lord to be shown to whom he was equal. God had given him to understand that he had not yet reached the level of a certain cobbler in Alexandria. Antony left the desert, went to the cobbler and asked him how he lived. His answer was that he gave a third of his income to the Church, another third to the poor, and kept the rest for himself. This did not seem a task out of the ordinary to Antony who himself had given up all his possessions and lived in the desert in total poverty. So that was not where the other man's superiority lay. Antony said to him, 'It is the Lord who has sent me to see how you live.' The humble tradesman, who venerated Antony, then told him his soul's secret: 'I do not do anything special. Only, as I work I look at all the passers-by and say, So that they may be saved, I, only I, will perish.'

We carry on doing our usual duties in the world but are

aware of the Divine at all times. This awareness results in compassion and permeates our attitudes and actions.

An essential tenet of early Christianity is that ordinary reality is interpenetrated with the Higher Reality: "Split the wood; I am there. Lift up the stone, and you will find me there." (Gospel of Thomas) Everything is in the Divine and the Divine is in everything. This is not pantheism, but panentheism: the Divine is both immanent and transcendent. The manifested reality gives shape to the Unmanifest.

But seeing the Divine in nature is more than that. It is seeing the visible universe give structure to the invisible. Apart from nature, geometry and music have often been used as a metaphor for the Divine: "Many ancient cultures chose to examine reality through the metaphors of geometry and music; they held the geometric-harmonic vision of universal order as being an interwoven configuration of wave patterns." (Robert Lawlor, *Sacred Geometry*)

In Taoist philosophy, too, there is the concept that the real things in the material world are a manifestation of a world of *archetypes (energetic patterns)*. This is very similar to Plato's *World of Ideas*, where objects we can see with our senses are expressions of transcendent concepts stored in our *nous,* our intuitive intelligence.

In the third level we leave ordinary time/space reality behind and perceive things we don't distinguish with our ordinary senses: "there we hear without hearing, see without seeing." (Meister

Eckhart) We are intuitively aware of the invisible, transcendent aspect of the Divine and are in union with it.

In describing the stages on the spiritual path we must keep two things in mind. Firstly that we are again talking of different levels of awareness. As we have already mentioned they do not develop in a linear fashion; we are not talking about a progression in time. The different levels occur simultaneously and develop in a spiral fashion deepening and overlapping.

Secondly, although the experience at heart may be an absolute and common human mystical experience, the different interpretations may give the illusion of diversity: some may stress the absence and others the presence of the Divine. This does not, however, negate the actual experience. Instead it does make us very conscious of the cultural and religious filters we use when trying to convey this experience in language.

In truly letting go of our images and expectations of our reality and the Ultimate Reality, we are temporarily faced by an imageless emptiness – the void. Slowly the realisation dawns that even this is one of our images shaped by our fear, and not the reality. The feeling of separation and aloneness is illusionary and will be replaced by an experience of being held in a sea of infinitely abundant richness and potential: Love.

Light

Yet as human beings we only comprehend reality through images. That is how our brain functions. But as long as we remain aware of the fact that the images we use to represent God are only shadows of the real, they are useful as tools for relating to God. They should not be used to restrict or determine our relationship.

The most common image used is Light, as we saw in the _Gospel of Thomas:_

Jesus said, "If they say to you, 'Where have you come from?' say to them, 'We have come from the light, from the place where the light came into being by itself, established itself ... We are its children, and we are the chosen of the living father.' If they ask you, 'What is the evidence of your father in you?' say to them, 'It is motion and rest.'"

This saying refers to a distinction often made by the mystics between God in creation _(motion)_ and the Godhead _(rest)_, the Source of All. We are made in the image and likeness of the Divine. Outwardly we manifest _God in motion_; inwardly we carry the Source of All in silence and stillness. But it also refers to the union of opposites, the non-dual nature of the Ultimate Reality.

Being

Apart from pure _Light_, God is experienced as pure _Being_ in the _Here and Now;_ "Among names none is more appropriate than He-who-is... for he dwells always anew in a Now without ceasing." (Meister Eckhart)

When Moses asks God who he is, he gets two answers – one stresses the historical, incarnated aspect – our images: "I am the God of Abraham, Isaac and Jacob" (Exodus) and the second points to the God we have been talking about: "I am that I am" (Exodus) – pure being, pure energy. In the *Gospel of John* we hear Jesus say something similar: "Before Abraham was 'I am'."

Therefore the only way we can get in touch with our Divine ground of being is by staying in the *Here and Now*. Eternity is in the *Now*. We need to realise that time is really made up out of a string of *Now* moments – everything happens in the *Now*. But we distort the *Now* by dwelling in our memories or by using this precious moment as a mere stepping stone to anticipate and prepare for the future.

Once the *Now* moment has been and gone, what is left of it is a mere memory. These are again constructs of the mind: interpretations of events coloured by self-deception, by fear, hope or the need for consolation, really not much different from a dream or fantasy.

This colouring furthermore varies depending on our changing moods and circumstances. We need to let go of these mirages; there is really only the *Here and Now*. Being present, listening attentively to the mantra enables us to do so, to let go of thoughts and images, the past and the future and allows us to be our true *self* dwelling in the *Now*.

We need to keep our attention single-mindedly on the *Here and Now* as is beautifully expressed in the poem of R.S. Thomas, *The Bright Field:*

> *I have seen the sun break through*

to illuminate a small field
for a while, and gone my way
and forgotten it. But that was the pearl
of great price, the one field that had
the treasure in it. I realize now
that I must give all that I have
to possess it. Life is not hurrying
onto a receding future, nor hankering after
an imagined past. It is the turning
aside like Moses to the miracle
of the lit bush, to a brightness
that seemed as transitory as your youth
once, but it is eternity that awaits you.

This *bright field* is, as Père de Caussade called it, "the sacrament of the present moment." We need to free ourselves of the linear, chronological notion of time in space/time – time as *Chronos* – this limited level of *ego* consciousness, and use one-pointed attention to stay in this *Moment* – time as *Cheiros* – the infinite, eternal *Now*.

Meditation makes this possible. This is the *narrow path* that leads to the Divine: a way of prayer that transcends all words and images, purified and poised awareness "trying to pass beyond that to a simple sense of presence, of waiting on God, of union with Him." (Bishop Kallistos)

God is Love

In many of the Wisdom traditions the Ultimate Reality and love are equated: "Every one who loves is a child of God and knows

God ... For God is love." (Gospel of John)

Bede Griffiths told the lovely story of how he felt at a loss when he had not died after his stroke. And then he heard a voice, saying *Surrender to the Mother* and he did. Then he felt as if penetrated by waves of Love. People who visited him afterwards said that he became an embodiment of love – the reserved Oxford English gentleman was gone.

In the *Chadogya Upanishads* too we read: "There is a Spirit that is mind and life, light and truth and vast spaces. He contains all works and desires and all perfumes and tastes. He enfolds the whole universe, and in silence is loving to all. This is the Spirit that is in my heart."

The only yardstick of progress in meditation is: *is there an increase in love for self and for others.* Having found God in our own depth, we find him everywhere. In Christianity 'union' with the Ultimate Reality is a relationship in love.

What drives us on, despite all difficulties on the path, is not an intellectual exercise but a longing that comes from our true *self*, a longing to return *home*: "Thou hast made us for Thyself, O God, and our hearts are restless till they rest in thee." (St Augustine)

And yet this longing is often obscured by fear, fear of the Unknown. The following story illustrates this beautifully:

Once upon a time, twin boys were conceived. Weeks passed and the twins developed. As their awareness grew, they laughed for joy: "Isn't it great that we were conceived? Isn't it great to be alive?"

Together the twins explored their world. When they found their mother's cord that gave them life, they sang for joy! "How great our mother love is, that she shares her own life with us!" As the weeks stretched into months, the twins noticed how much each was changing. "What does it mean?" one asked. "It means our stay in this world is drawing to an end," said the other. "But I don't want to go," said one. "I want to stay here always." "We have no choice," said the other. "But maybe there is life after birth." "But how can that be?" responded one. "We will shed our life cord and how can life be possible without it? Besides, we have seen evidence that others were here before us, and none of them has returned to tell us there is life after birth. No, this is the end. Maybe there is no mother after all." "But there has to be," protested the other. "How else did we get here? How do we remain alive?" "Have you seen our mother?" said one. "Maybe she only lives in our minds. Maybe we made her up because the idea made us feel good." So the last days in the womb were filled with deep questioning and fear. Finally, the moment of birth arrived. When the twins had passed from their world, they opened their eyes and cried for joy – for what they saw exceeded their fondest dreams.

That is birth …and that is death. (Unknown author)

We fear extinction, we fear death. But there is no need to be afraid. The one expression that is most used in spiritual teaching is:

Do not be afraid

We hear it so many times in Christian Scriptures and see it

in Hindu and Buddhist statues in the hand gesture:

Abhaya! Fear not!

Meditation helps us to release fear and grow in love.

Dancing with your Shadow is precisely that: accepting in joy and fearless love all aspects of the *Self* and integrating them into a harmonious, cooperative whole – thus becoming part of the Dance of the Universe.

Wisdom is recognising the rhythm of the Cosmos.
Joy is dancing to this Rhythm.

EPILOGUE:

The Roots of Christian Meditation

Meditation is an ancient way of prayer in the Christian tradition, although it sometimes feels as if it is the world's best kept secret. It does not replace our ordinary ways of prayer; it is considered to be complementary, deepening and completing the whole of the spiritual discipline of prayer:

"Meditation is the missing dimension of much Christian life today. It does not exclude other types of prayer and indeed deepens reverence for the sacraments and scripture." (Laurence Freeman)

The spiritual aspect of Christianity seems to have been largely forgotten. Recovery of this spiritual dimension, however, is essential:

"If Christianity cannot recover its mystical tradition and teach it, it should just fold up and go out of business, it has nothing to say." (Fr Bede Griffiths)

At the heart of all the great world religions is the *spiritual* experience of one person, Jesus, the Buddha, Mohammed. On that original spiritual experience and the teaching flowing from it the disciples of that teacher after his death then base a religion. But trying to capture the true spirit of this experience in words is very difficult. We end up with the words, the thoughts of these great teachers, filtered through the cultural, mental, psychological, emotional frame work of the listener.

This was also the case with the early Christians. We saw the influence of Plato as well as the influence of the Stoic ethics and the teaching of Moses. Even if people of that time personally had not studied Greek or Jewish philosophy, it formed the background to their thinking in the same way that the Cartesian or the quantum view of reality unconsciously forms ours, as we have seen. Judging by the impact he had on people, Jesus was quite a charismatic person. But people heard what would fit into their worldview, what resonated with them. The questions – who he was, why he had come, what his meaning was – were answered against this background. The result was that there were various differing interpretations; there were about 80 distinct Christian groupings soon after Christ's resurrection, beginning with groups around some of the apostles. Consequently there were many gospels, interpretations and accounts of Jesus' life. Each of them had an individual bias, saying rather more about the followers and their audience than about Jesus and his teaching.

Furthermore, Christianity and Judaism were monotheistic – unlike the Roman and other religions surrounding them. As they believed that there was only one God it mattered how they related to that God. Therefore in Christianity what they believed became all important, in fact it determined whether they were saved or not.

At this early stage of Christianity there were few bishops, no creeds and no accepted canon of Scripture. This was the problem facing the Christian leaders after the demise of the apostles. It was difficult to determine what the true teaching was. Moreover, the life of the early Christians was stamped by the experience of persecution and martyrdom under the Roman Empire. Christians were persecuted for their refusal to honour other gods. The Jews were not prepared to do this either, but theirs was an ancient religion that made this attitude acceptable.

Christianity was seen as a recent troublesome faction that conflicted with the norms of Roman culture and society. Christians were considered a strange sect and were opposed with all the suspicions and prejudices that we still exhibit when faced with cults or sects we don't understand.

Sometimes the troubles were started by the Roman Emperor or a Roman official; at other times ordinary citizens mobbed and killed Christians. And yet their courageous behaviour and moral integrity under this persecution resulted in many pagans being inspired and converted. This happened to Pachomius, a Roman soldier, who went on to become a desert monk founding the first large monastic communities in the desert.

St Ireneaus, Bishop of Lyons, and the Christians there were badly affected by the persecution and death of martyrs in 177. When the surviving ones heard of Christians fighting with Christians in Rome, they sent Irenaeus to speak to the Pope to resolve the issue.

When Irenaeus went to Rome, he encountered the

Montanists, a very popular charismatic group that spoke of new prophecies, saw visions and dreamed dreams. They were led by Montanus and two women, Maximilia and Priscilla. The latter claimed that Christ had appeared to her in the shape of a woman. Their popularity was a divisive force amongst the Christians of that time – the cause of the above mentioned in-fighting.

The difficulty with visions is to discern whether they come from the Spirit or from the delusions of the *ego*. Since the Montanists perceived themselves as spirit-led, they claimed that their knowledge of Christ was genuine and came to them directly. In doing so they indirectly attacked the authority of the Church and that meant Irenaeus' own authority.

However dismayed Ireneaus may have been by the popularity of this group, they were basically 'orthodox'. Christianity from the beginning was very much spirit-led with dreams, visions and prophecy playing a major part. The annunciation of Mary was by an angel; Joseph was told through dreams what to do; Jesus heard words and saw a dove at his baptism and underwent temptations in the desert.

But the ones considered much more dangerous by Ireneaus were those disparate groups he gathered under the umbrella term of *Gnostics*. The most prominent group, whose leader was Valentinus, appeared to be close to mainstream teaching; they attended the same churches, read the same scriptures but interpreted them not literally but allegorically. These were often "the most faithful, wisest and most experienced members of the

Christian churches." (Tertullian) But they too relied on spirit-led *gnosis,* direct intuitive *knowledge.*

Valentinus (ca.105-165 A.D.) was educated in Alexandria and went to Rome in 136 A.D. He was so popular that he narrowly missed being made Bishop of Rome. Even in our time Gilles Quispel, a scholar of Gnosticism, said that reading Valentinus during the Second World War gave him such hope, faith and consolation. But again Valentinus' followers exaggerated and twisted his teachings. Some other Gnostic groupings were quite extreme in their dualistic views.

In an attempt to create some order amongst these disparate groups, St Ireneaus decided to select four gospels as orthodox, meaning *right thinking,* as the canon, the guideline: Matthew, Mark, Luke and John and of course the letters of St Paul.

He chose John rather than Thomas – although the latter was very popular – because Irenaeus' teacher Polycarp had been a follower of John. Irenaeus could therefore claim the all-important apostolic succession. Moreover the two gospels were very similar.

Every other gospel – and the group who used them – were considered heretic, which means literally *someone who chooses.* Some of these also had an apostolic pedigree, but Ireneaus felt the line had to be drawn somewhere.[1]

From then on two different strands appeared in Christianity: one stressed pure faith and literal belief in the agreed scriptures

---

[1] I am indebeted to Elaine Pagels, Bart Eherman and Karen King for this background. (See Bibliography)

as the only criteria for being a true Christian and the other one felt that this was not enough. They stressed the importance of going deeper and thus acquiring intuitive knowledge of God through Spirit-led insights and experiences.

The first strand was to become the 'orthodox' aspect of Christianity. This approach was addressed at that time to the more unlettered, with an emphasis on an unreflective acceptance of a set of beliefs, encouragement of highly moral behaviour and a rejection of any intellectual approach – especially involving any metaphorical interpretation of scripture.

To the second strand, spirituality, the contemplative force, was integral to their Christianity. These included often the more questioning intellectual Christians brought up on a diet of Plato et al, who may even have been open enough to dialogue with Buddhist and Hindu philosophy. We know that Pantaenus, Clement of Alexandria's teacher, did so. Ireneaus considered this grouping *heretic, gnostic*, in the pejorative sense of *know-it alls*.

Since the *orthodox* believers in later centuries laid the foundations of the Church as it has come to us over the ages, spirituality has ever since then been considered with suspicion:

"Perhaps this is why most religious institutions, jealous of their authority, have suspected or tried to control the contemplative force. Whenever they have succeeded, religion itself has been damaged because it is contemplation that authenticates the way religion witnesses to truth and revelation." (Laurence Freeman)

The result of this is that religion and spirituality are considered to be separate – even nowadays opposed – entities. But of course they are integrally connected: "If religion is the prose of the soul then spirituality is its poetry." (Chief Rabbi Jonathan Sachs)

To separate the two creates an imbalance that has severe repercussion on religion itself:

"Religion is a sacred expression of the spiritual, but if the spiritual experience is lacking then the religious form becomes hollow, superficial and self-important." (John Main)

Ireneaus' attempt in the 2nd century to unify Christians in this way did not really bear fruit. It resulted in even more splinter groups for the next two centuries. However, in the fourth century there was an important turn of events. The Emperor Constantine granted freedom of worship to the Christians in 312, but this did not necessarily make the situation easier for everyone. Constantine favoured the largest and best organised 'orthodox' group of bishops for his own reasons. He penalised all the other churches that had different interpretations of Jesus and his teaching. On these groups he imposed extra taxes and demanded more public duties from them.

Athanasius, Bishop of Alexandria, a Copt, belonging to those who favoured a literal approach, was now empowered to insist on the canon already mentioned by Irenaeus. Apart from the four accepted gospels, all alternative gospels were to be destroyed.

Unlike Ireneaus, Athanasius was successful as he had the backing of the Emperor Constantine.

Money pouring into the Christian movement was an added problem. Many churches were built with Imperial money. It became a lucrative business to be a Christian leader:

"Plagues teeming with untold mischief have come upon the churches. The primary offices have become marketable. Excessive wealth, enormous power and luxury are destroying the integrity of the Church." (St John Chrysostom, *Homilies in Ephesus*)

This was near the end of the Roman civilisation – a very decadent period. Once more we hear St John Chrysostom on the attack this time against the immorality of his time, especially that of the upper classes "their softly nurtured flesh draped only in heavy jewelry." Even monks and nuns were definitely not beyond reproach. Clergy were even accused of sorcery.

The Desert Fathers and Mothers

In reaction, men and women retired to the silence and solitude of the Desert in search of the opportunity to experience an authentic spiritual life, as they felt they could no longer do so in the ordinary world of the Roman Empire. They wanted to lead a life according to the Gospel, using ancient forms of monasticism. Living in the presence of God – *enlightenment* – was the ultimate aim and achieving *purity of heart* was the way.

They saw going into the desert and leading this life of poverty and deprivation as a kind of martyrdom, a *white* martyrdom as opposed to the *red* martyrdom of the real martyrs, who were deeply venerated. They gave up all that for most of us forms the essence of life; they were rebels who went against the accepted norms of their time and did not consider that owning property, being married, having a role in society was essential to leading a meaningful life.

The saying of Paul: "Do not model yourself on the behaviour of the world around you, but let your behaviour change, modelled by your new mind." (Romans 12:2) was their guiding thought. They regarded society "as a shipwreck from which each individual man had to swim for his life." (Thomas Merton)

They were certainly not the first hermits in the Desert – Antony visited several in the beginning of his journey and Pachomius was trained by the anchorite Palamon. But there had never been so many of them. First there were only a few, but by the end of the 4th century there were at least thirty thousands monks and nuns living in the deserts of Egypt, Palestine and Syria.

The Desert Fathers and Mothers would have been influenced by all the different groups that existed at the time. Since the Coptic monks were 'gentiles', the teaching of St Paul was very influential; but there were many other gospels in circulation, to which they would have had access. Some of the monks may even have been 'Gnostics'. This was proved in 1945 when a large vase with many ancient manuscripts was found near Nag Hammadi, very close to the monastery established by Pachomius in the 4th century. It does not seem unlikely that the monks there treasured these writings and were reluctant to destroy them as ordered by Athanasius and buried them instead. It contained works attributed to Valentinus and other Gnostic writers, but also gospels of other apostles, including the *Gospel of Thomas*, a collection of sayings compiled from the oral tradition of the first century.

The Desert Fathers were not a homogeneous group:

"Abba Poemen said that Abba John said that the saints are like a group of trees, each bearing different fruit but watered from the same source. The practices of one saint differ from those of another, but it is the same Spirit that works in all of them." (Sayings of the Desert Fathers)

We again find both mystically inclined groups and anti-mystical groups. On the one hand we have the educated *Origenist* monks with their *neo-platonic* belief in the soul's affinity to God and the possibility of its ascent to and union with a *nameless and ineffable* God and probably Gnostic monks. On the other hand we have the more literally minded simple Coptic monks who acquired their biblical knowledge orally, as many of them were illiterate, and had an anthropomorphic image of God. To the latter, as for Athanasius, there was an unbridgeable gulf between God and humankind. Only a life of repentance and struggle against the powers of evil, trying to defeat the demons on their own ground, may allow God's grace to cross this divide to save them, hence Athanasius' emphasis in his *Life of Antony* on Antony's struggle with the demons rather than his ascent to the Divine.

However these differences between the two groups were only

on the rational surface level. In the depth their teaching was identical, as it was in both cases based on the practical experience of their life of prayer in the Desert. Both stressed purifying the desires – fighting the *demons* and thus clarifying the mind and freeing it from the drives of the *ego*. The deep psychological insights we find in their sayings are a reflection of this lived experience. The way to this *purification* was *detachment,* not only from thoughts involving ourselves – also important to the Coptic monks – but for the *Origenist* monks even thoughts, words and images about God. They were convinced that the Divine cannot be encompassed in this way. They would have totally agreed with the statement of Wittgenstein: "What we cannot speak about, we must pass over in silence."

To help them to detach from thoughts and other distractions and silence the mind they used a *formula* – we call that now a mantra – a prayer phrase that they repeated: "Let the mind hold ceaselessly to this formula ... until it renounces and rejects the whole abundance of thought." (John Cassian, *Conferences*)

Cassian recommended the phrase: "O God make speed to save us; O Lord make haste to help us." He recommended that the use of the mantra should not be restricted only to times of meditation, but he encouraged having it continually in mind: "You should, I say, meditate constantly on this verse in your heart...You should not stop repeating it when you are doing any kind of work or performing some service or are on a journey. Meditate on it while sleeping and eating and attending to the least needs of nature." Their intention was to acquire *continual prayer* as recommended in the Gospels.

They stressed that meditation with a mantra led to pure contemplation without conscious awareness: "The monk who knows that he is praying is not praying, but the monk who does not know he is praying is praying." (St Antony)

The simple life the desert hermits led in the silence and solitude of the desert supported their efforts to reach this deep interior stillness and silence. They left all possessions behind and lived in caves or simple dwellings devoting their life to reaching the Ultimate Reality. They ate frugally and provided themselves with the essentials by making baskets or ropes to sell in the market. The starkness of the desert formed the background to the simplicity of their life. They just did what was absolutely necessary for staying alive; they considered anything else as being done out of motives of the *ego*, and therefore to go counter to the aim of reaching pure awareness. Their simple life also resulted in less anxiety and consequently fewer distracting thoughts at the time of meditation.

People are often surprised when Desert Mothers are mentioned; however, there were many women in the Desert. These were even braver than their male counterparts in going against social convention; at that time a woman had no rights and was considered a chattel of her father and later her husband. Their life cannot have been easy in the desert. They will have come across prejudice without doubt by many, including some of their fellow hermits, but the Christian leaders of the time supported them, as we see in the following saying: "Woman is in the image of God equally with man. The sexes are of equal worth. Their virtues are equal, their struggles are equal … Would a man be able to compete with a woman who lives her life to the full?" (Gregory of Nyssa 335-398)

The Desert Tradition was an oral teaching, and the pithy advice of both genders had been recorded by their disciples in various manuscripts. The manuscript of the *Meterikon*, the sayings of the mothers, has not survived. We only have some of their sayings mentioned in the *Apophtegmata, The Sayings of the Fathers*. By being written down and collected in these manuscripts the sayings lose an important aspect: originally these sayings were specific advice meant for one individual. This context is lost.

The *going underground* of the *spiritual* tradition

This teaching was made known in the Christian West by John Cassian, who had totally absorbed the teaching of his beloved Desert Fathers. He himself was an *Origenist* monk, his main teacher being Evagrius. His *Conferences* are a record of conversations held with at least fifteen Desert Fathers in different places and times in the Egyptian Desert near Alexandria. This vast work shows the goal of the desert hermits: to reach union with the Ultimate Reality by obtaining *purity of heart.* Cassian elaborates on and explains Evagrius' teaching, which basically he does not alter but phrases more diplomatically.

The diplomacy was necessary after Evagrius' death, as his teaching as well as Origen's, were by that time considered *heretical,* a direct result of the clashes between the different Christian groupings, between the Coptic monks and the *Origenist* monks. The latter were being chased out of the desert by the Coptic monks in 400 A.D., a year after the death of Evagrius.

This is the decisive moment when the *spiritual* interpretation of Christianity in the West lost out. St Augustine, who was also very influenced by the Desert teaching, still married in his approach the *spiritual* and the *orthodox.* But like St Athanasius before him he stressed the gulf between God and sinful humanity. Only God's grace could bridge this gulf and save individuals.

St Benedict still recommended his monks to read Cassian daily, but after that this *spiritual* teaching and praying with a *formula,* a mantra, only surfaced here and there up to the 16th century in important mystics e.g. Francisco de Osuna, a strong influence on St Teresa of Avila, the anonymous writer of *The Cloud of Unknowing* and Augustine Baker, to mention just a few. After the Reformation and Counter-reformation, it disappeared from view until our century.

The Eastern Orthodox Tradition

In the East, however, another branch of this spiritual tradition with the same roots in the desert survived: the teaching of *Hesychasm* in the Eastern Orthodox Church. The writings of the Fathers of the Eastern Christian Tradition dating from the 4th to the 14th century were collected together in the *Philokalia*. There they stressed the repetition of the *Jesus Prayer* to reach the transformative stillness and silence. They called this type of prayer *The Prayer of the Heart,* and emphasized the movement from the rational mind to the deeper intuitive heart: "Collect your mind into your heart and send out thence your mental cry to our Lord Jesus, calling for his help and saying 'Lord Jesus Christ, have mercy upon me." (St Gregory of Sinai)

This tradition became known in the West in the 19th Century through the delightful anonymous book *The Way of the Pilgrim.*

John Main

John Main, a Benedictine monk, had been taught to pray with a mantra by Swami Satyananda, a Rama Krishna monk he met when he was serving in the British Colonial Service in Malaysia in the course of his duties there. He was a practising Christian then, but it was still many years before he became a monk himself.

Much later John Main discovered the way that he had been taught to pray in Malaysia in the writings of John Cassian.[2] We can no doubt imagine the joy he must have felt that this praying with a mantra, from which he had derived such benefit, was also part of the ancient Christian Tradition.

---

[2] For a detailed account of John Main's discovery of mantra meditation in Christianity, please see *The Gethsemani Talks.*

His essential contribution is that he made known this way of prayer in our time and stressed that it was not only for monks and nuns, but for anyone.

This way of prayer fulfills a real need. Surprisingly there are many similarities between our time and that of the Desert Fathers and Mothers. Since the early 60s, many of us have experienced a similar thirst for spirituality. An alternative way of living has also been advocated, rejecting the prevalent materialistic, hedonistic culture. The Church in which people were brought up is also sometimes rejected as lacking real value and spirituality.

John Main's teaching on meditation is, like the Desert Tradition, firmly rooted in the teaching of Jesus. His emphasis, like theirs, was never on theory, dogma or doctrine, but on the experience itself and the discipline this required.

"And during the time of your meditation there must be in your mind no thoughts, no words, and no imaginations. The sole sound will be the sound of your mantra, your word. The mantra ... is like a harmonic. And as we sound this harmonic within ourselves we begin to build up a resonance. That resonance then leads us forward to our own wholeness ... We begin to experience the deep unity we all posses in our own being. And then the harmonic begins to build up a resonance between you and all creatures and all creation and a unity between you and your Creator." (John Main)

For more than 20 years his successor Laurence Freeman OSB has tirelessly travelled the world to spread the knowledge of the re-discovery of this tradition which is now practised in more than 40 countries. The World Community for Christian Meditation is an ecumenical community and has been in dialogue with other Christian denominations and other world religions, in particular with Buddhism and HH the Dalai Lama.

APPENDIX I
The scriptural evidence

The Desert tradition was based on the teaching of Jesus as expressed in the Gospels. But Christians often wonder where it says in Christian Scripture that meditation is an acceptable way on the Spiritual path. It would be good to be able to refer to a passage where it is stated in so many words, but that is unfortunately not possible. But the essentials of Christian meditation are there for all to see: *silence, stillness, interiority, no thoughts, emphasis on few words, repetition, solitude, alertness, staying in the present moment, one-pointed attention and union.*

Importance of silence

Ps 46:10   *Be still and know that I am God*

Ps 131:1-2   *Truly I have set my soul in silence and in Peace... A weaned child on its mother's breast even so is my soul.*

Zach 2 14-15/17   *Let all mankind be silent before the Lord, for he is awakening and is coming from his holy dwelling.*

1Kings 19:12   *a still small voice*

Interiority/ indwelling spirit

Mat 6, 6   *But when you pray, go into your room, shut the door, and pray to your father, who is there in the secret place; and your Father who sees what is secret will reward you.*

Luke 17, 20 21   *You cannot tell by observation when the Kingdom of God comes. There will be no saying, 'Look, here it is!' Or 'There it is!' for in fact the Kingdom of God is within you.*

1 Cor 3,16   *Surely you know that you are God's temple, where the Spirit of God dwells.*

Ephesians 1:17-18   *I pray that the God of our Lord Jesus Christ, the all-glorious Father, may give you the spiritual powers of wisdom and vision, by which there comes knowledge him. I pray that your inward eyes may be illumined.*

Ephesians 3:16-17   *he may grant you strength and power through his Spirit in your inner being that through faith Christ may dwell in your hearts in love. Few words/poverty of spirit*

Matt 6:7-8   *In your prayers do not go babbling on like the heathen, who imagine that the more they say the more likely they are to be heard.*

Luke 18: 10-14   *Prayer of the the tax-gatherer 'O God, have mercy on me, sinner that I am.'*

Ceaseless prayer

Thess 5:17   *Pray continually*

Romans 12:12   *persist in prayer*

Luke 18   *they should persist in prayer and never lose heart* (also Matt 11:5-11)

Importance of solitude

Luke 6:12   *During this time he went out one day into the hills to pray and spent the night in prayer to God.*

Alertness

Mark 13:33   *Be alert, be wakeful*

✳ Matt 25:1-13   *Keep awake then; for you never know the day or the hour. . . Stay in the present moment*

Matt 6, 25   *Therefore I bid you put away anxious thoughts about food and drink to keep you alive, and clothes to cover your body.*
✳ *Surely life is more than food, the body more than clothes.*

Silencing of thoughts/leaving self-consciousness behind

Luke 9:23   *If anyone wishes to be a follower of mine, he must leave self behind.*

Humility and trust

TURN AROUND

Matt 18:1-4   *I tell you this: unless you turn around and become like children, you will never enter the Kingdom of Heaven.*

Unity with God and with others/wholeness

John 17, 21   *may they all be one; as Thou, Father, art in me and I in Thee, so also may they be one in us.*

John 10:10- 11   *I have come that men may have life, and may have it in all its fullness.*

One pointed focus on the 'Presence' of God

Matt 6, 33   *Set your mind on God's Kingdom and his Justice before everything else and all the rest will come to you as well"*

Ps 116:8   *I will walk in the Presence of the Lord in the land of the living.*

Matt 5:3   *How blest are those who know their need of God; the Kingdom of Heaven is theirs.*

Matt 5:   *How blest are those whose heart are pure they shall see God.*

APPENDIX II

Preparation for meditation

Let me remind you of the actual practice of meditation:
Sit down. Sit still and upright. Close your eyes lightly. Sit relaxed but alert. Silently, interiorly begin to say a single word. Listen to it as you say it, gently but continuously. Do not think or imagine anything spiritual or otherwise. If thoughts and images come, these are distractions at the time of meditation, so keep returning to simply saying the word. Meditate twenty to thirty minutes each morning and evening.

This sounds simple but it is not easy! There a few preparatory exercises which may help to get your body, mind and spirit in the right framework.

There are three aspects to be considered:

• The body
• The breath
• The mind

Stilling the body

The moment we try to sit still and at ease, we become aware of how tense we really are. To help the body to relax, it is paradoxically helpful to become aware of all sense impressions in our body. The following exercise may be helpful:

Put all your attention on your scalp, a major carrier of stress;

put your total concentration on what you can feel in your scalp. You may want to move your eyebrows or your ears to become aware that you actually do have a scalp. Focus all your awareness there. How does it feel? What can you feel? Can you feel anything? Become your scalp. Breathe in gently and breathe out and let go of all tension and stress there. Put your scalp at ease. Gently repeat this several times, always breathing in gently and breathing out long and relaxed and let go.

Now put your attention on your face, especially on the frowning points between the eyebrows, around the nose and mouth. We tend to frown, pinch our nose and purse our lips more than we know. Put all of your attention there. Become aware of what you do. Move the muscles in your face. It doesn't matter. No one is looking. Now really frown, scrunch up your face. Then widen your face relaxing the muscles. The half smile we see on the Buddha's face is not a smile as such, but a totally relaxed face. Breathe in gently and let go off all the tension in your face. Just breathe out and let go. Breathing in gently and breathing out long, relaxed and let go.

Now put all your awareness on your mouth, tongue and jaws. Where is your tongue? Is it against the roof of your mouth? This is a sure sign of tension and readiness to talk. Let it drop. Let it fall gently to where it naturally wants to be. Are your jaws clenched? Let them go. Put your awareness on the point where your jaws are connected, just under your ears. Put all your awareness there and breathe in gently and breathe out and let go.

Just let them go. The mouth is closed but totally relaxed.

Once more check your scalp, your face, your tongue, and your jaws.

Now put your awareness on your shoulders. How do they feel? Move them up and down to become aware of how you hold them. Breathe in gently and breathe them down. It is amazing, how far down they will go. Just keep your awareness there and breathe out and let go.

How is your neck? Does it feel relaxed? Look up at the ceiling by tilting your head back, slowly as if against some resistance, then let it drop forward totally relaxed and free. Do this two more times and during the last one instead of letting your head drop forward, let the back of your neck grow and grow. Without having done anything else your chin will be gently tucked in and as the Fathers of the Eastern Christian tradition said then your beard will tickle your chest. Then the neck is at ease, gently in line with your spine.

Check your posture now. Are you balanced? Do you feel really grounded on your chair or on the floor? No need to fight gravity, just relax and trust and let go. Every time you breathe out, think of roots growing down into the earth from you. Take your time to ground your self. And then think of your spine like a flower growing up to the sun. Two opposite movements are happening: down with gravity and up towards the light.

If the head and shoulders are at ease, the rest of the body will follow. But check for any tension in your arms and legs, especially the calves of your legs. Our legs work all the time and often we hold them tensed and ready to move, even when it is not necessary. Just tense and then relax the muscles of the parts of your arms and legs in rolling succession, constantly with total awareness. Every time your attention goes, just gently bring it back to whatever part of the body you are focusing on, breathing in gently and breathing out and letting go.

Check once more in your own time and at your own speed right over your body from your scalp to your feet. Put your body at ease. If there is any pain or discomfort, put your whole awareness there. Feel the pain. How does it feel, burning, nagging, or sharp? Really become aware of it, acknowledge it, then breathe in gently to that spot and then breathe out and let go. Just let go.

Become aware of your breath, which should be calm and gentle by now. You are relaxed but alert. Now take up your mantra and let it float on the breath, gently saying it in your mind to the rhythm of your breath, if this works for you. Otherwise let go of the breath and just say your word.

Stilling the breath

Focusing on the breath is the best way I know of leaving the world outside alone and turning within. Let's focus on the breath. Let's really get to know our breath. Put your attention on the breath at the nostrils. Feel it coming in cool and feel it going out warm: just focus on the sensations near the nostrils. Feel the air passing over the hairs in your nostrils. Don't alter your breath, just watch it, coming in cool and going out warm. Just breathe.

Now let's take your awareness of the breath a little further. Feel the breath cool at the back of your throat as you breathe in and warm as you breathe out. Just feel it coming in your nostrils and passing at the back of your throat, cool coming in and warm going out. Just breathe.

Now let's take the awareness of the breath a little further still. Feel it going into your heart region. Notice the top of your chest moving slightly, feel the air going in and going out: your chest going up and going down. You might even feel your heart beating. Just focus your whole attention on the air going in and going out. Just breathe.

Now let's go even deeper. Feel the air filling the bottom of your lungs. Feel your lower ribcage expanding and contracting. Just enjoy the movement of your ribcage. Just breathe.

Now let's go even deeper. Your diaphragm is like an upturned cup. When you breathe in, the diaphragm goes down and the cup flattens and becomes a upturned saucer. And when you breathe out, it goes up and back to its upturned cup shape. Breathe in, going down and flattening, breathing out and going up. Just focus all your awareness on your diaphragm moving up and down. Just breathe.

Now just breathe naturally and watch your breathing. How does it feel? Where can you feel the breath?

Now don't alter your breath, just breathe in and out naturally.

Both these exercises are excellent ways to settle down for meditation. These exercises should only take you 5 minutes; a bit more or less depending on how used you are to doing this and how tense you are at this moment. Stilling the body and the breath are not done for their own sake. Only when the body and the breath are still and at ease can we leave it alone for the time of our meditation. It is difficult to focus, when your body is uncomfortable, demanding your attention.

Watching the thoughts

Watching the mind from a distance as if dealing with some one else' experiences, as if it is all only a play, stops the tendency to identify totally with the products of our mind. Just pay your thoughts some dispassionate attention; just watch them following one another, totally chaotic, one association after another. But don't get hooked by any thought. You are not interested in the whys and wherefores. If it helps, just name them. In that way you get to know what you are like at this moment, and that it is alright to be like that. Befriend the part of you that is your thoughts. It is a way of learning to accept yourself with all your preoccupations.

Sometimes there is a dominant recurring thought, which just won't let you be. Focus all your attention on it; acknowledge it without being hooked by it. What does it feel like? Heavy, light? What shape has it? What is the feeling associated with it? There is a close connection between thoughts, feelings and your body. Where is that feeling located in your body? If it had a colour, what would it be? If we had to represent it as a sound, which one would be appropriate? What sensations are associated with it? Is there an image that springs to mind? Really get to know that recurring thought and feeling; give it all your attention and befriend it. Then when you feel you know it, let it go. Tell it you will attend to it after this period of meditation. By really getting to know it in this way, we actually detach ourselves from it. We are not exploring the causes of thoughts, but looking at their effects objectively.

BIBLIOGRAPHY

Anonymous author, *Meditation on the Tarot* (Tarcher/Putnam)

Anonymous author, *The Way of the Pilgrim* (Triangle)

Bohm, David, *Wholeness and the Implicate Order* (Routledge)

Blake, William, *The Poems of William Blake* (Serate)

Capra, Fritjof, *The Tao of Physics* (Flamingo)

Cassian, John, *The Conferences* (Paulist Press)

Ehrman, Bart D, *Lost Christianities* (Oxford University Press)

Evagrius Ponticus, *The Praktikos & Chapters on Prayer* (Cistercian Publications)

Ferrucci, Piero, *What We May Be* (Tarcher/Putnam)

Freeman, Laurence, *Jesus, the Teacher Within* (Continuum)

   The Selfless Self (D.L.T)

   Aspects of Love

Fromm, Erich, *Psychoanalysis and Religion* (Bantam Books)

Griffiths, Bede, *A New Vision of Reality* (Fount)

   The Marriage of East and West (Fount)

Huxley, Aldous, *The Perennial Philosophy* (Harper&Row)

King, Karen L., *What is Gnosticism?* (Harvard University Press)

Lao Tzu, *Tao Te Ching* translated by Stephen Mitchell (Frances Lincoln)

Main, John, *Word into Silence* (D.L.T.)

   The Gethsemani Talks (Medio Media)

   Monastery Without Walls (Canterbury Press)

Merton, Thomas, *The Wisdom of the Desert* (Darley Anderson, London)

   The Way of Chuang Tzu (New Directions)

McTaggart, Lynne, *The Field* (Element)

Origen, *The Classics of Western Spirituality* (Paulist Press)

Pagels, Elaine, *Beyond Belief: The Secret Gospel of Thomas* (Macmillan)

The Philokalia – The complete text – Volume one (Faber & Faber)

On Prayer of the Heart (Faber & Faber)

Storr, Anthony, *The Essential Jung* (Fontana Press)

Tolle, Eckhart, *The Power of Now* (Hodder and Stoughton)

Ward, Sr Benedicta SLG, *Sayings of the Desert Fathers:*
  The Alphabetical Collection
  The Wisdom of the Desert Fathers

Wilber, Ken, *A Brief History of Everything* (Gill & MacMillan Ltd)
  No Boundary (Shambala)
  Up from Eden (Quest Books)

ABOUT THE WORLD COMMUNITY
FOR CHRISTIAN MEDITATION

The World Community for Christian Meditation took form in 1991. It continues John Main's legacy in teaching Christian meditation and his work of restoring the contemplation dimension of Christian faith in the life of the church.

The Community is now directed by Laurence Freeman OSB, a student of John Main and a Benedictine monk of the Olivetan Congregation. The World Community has its International Centre and a retreat centre in London. There are a number of Centres in other parts of the world. The Community is thus a "monastery without walls", a family of national communities and emerging communities in over a hundred countries. The foundation of this Community is the local meditation group, which meets weekly in homes, parishes, offices, hospitals, prisons, and colleges. The World Community works closely with many Christian churches.

Annually it runs the John Main Seminar and The Way of Peace. It also sponsors retreats, schools for the training of teachers of meditation seminars, lectures, and other programs. It contributes to interfaith dialogues particularly, in recent years with Buddhists and Muslims. A quarterly spiritual letter with news of the community is mailed and also available online. Weekly readings can be sent direct by email. Information on current programmes, connections to national coordinators and the location of meditation groups can be found on the Community website www.wccm.org which also offers a range of online audio talks. This site is the hub of a growing family of internet presence, the web sites of national communities and special interests, such as the teaching of meditation to children and the contemporary spirituality of priests.

Medio Media is the communication and publishing arm of The World Community and offers a wide range of books, audio and videos to support the practice of meditation. The online bookstore is at www.mediomedia.org.

THE WORLD COMMUNITY FOR CHRISTIAN MEDITATION

CENTRES/CONTACTS WORLDWIDE

International Centre
WCCM
St Mark's
Myddelton Square
London
EC1R 1XX
Tel: +44 20 7278 2070
Fax: +44 20 7713 6346
Email: mail@wccm.org
         www.wccm.org

FOR COUNTRIES NOT LISTED
CONTACT INTERNATIONAL CENTRE

Australia
Australian Christian Meditation Community
PO Box 246
Uralla
New South Wales 2358
Tel: +61 2 9904 4638
E-mail: palmy@ozemail.com.au
www.christianmeditationaustralia.org

Belgium
Christelijk Meditatie Centrum
Beiaardlaan 1
B-1850 Grimbergen
Tel/Fax: +32 2 305 7513
Email: ccm@pandora.be
         www.clik.to/ccmbe

Brazil
Comunidade de Meditacao Crista
Caixa postal 62559
CEP 22252 Rio de Janeiro
Brasil
Tel: +55 21 2523 5125
Email: **ana.fonseca@umusic.com**
www.wccm.com.br

Canada
Christian Meditation Community
Canadian National Resource Centre
P.O. Box 552, Station NDG
Montreal, Quebec
H4A 3P9
Tel: +1 514 485 7928
Fax: +1 514 489 9899
Email: meditatio@sympatico.ca
         www.meditatio.ca

Méditation Chretiénne du Québec
7400 boul. St. Laurent, Suite 526
Montréal, Québec H2R 2Y1
Tel: +1 514 525 4649
Fax: +1 514 525 8110
Email: medchre@bellnet.ca

Fiji
Christian Meditation Centre
PO Box 3340
Lami
Tel: +679 361106
Fax: +679 361181
Email: frdenis@relpac.org.fj

France
Communauté Mondiale de Méditants Chrétiens
126 rue Pelleport
75020 Paris
Tel: +33 1 40 31 89 73
Email: cmmc@wanadoo.fr

Germany
WCCM
Untere Leiten 12 d
82065 Baierbrunn
Tel: +49 89 68020914
Fax: +49 89 74424917
Email: hm.plotzki@gmx.de
        www.wccm.de

India
Christian Meditation Centre
Kripa Foundation
Mt Carmel Church
81/A Chapel Road
Bandra (W)
Mumbai 400050
Tel: +91 22 640 5411
Fax: +91 22 643 9296
Email: frjoe@bom5.vsnl.net.in

Ireland
Christian Meditation Centre
4 Eblana Avenue
Dun Laoghaire
Co. Dublin
Tel: +353 1 280 1505
Fax: +353 1 280 8720
e-mail: mclougf@hotmail.com
www.wccmireland.org

Italy
Comunità Mondiale per la Meditazione Cristiana
Via Marche, 2/a
25125 Brescia
Tel: +39 030 224549
e-mail: wccmitalia@virgilio.it
www.meditazionecristiana.org

Malaysia
The World Community for Christian Meditation
1439 Jalan 17/21-L
46400 Petaling Jaya
Selangor
Tel: +60 3 79587050
Fax: +60 3 79545780
Email: ppor@pc.jaring.my

New Zealand
Christian Meditation Community
PO Box 15-402
Tauranga
Tel: +64 7 544 7955
Email: stanman@xtra.co.nz

Philippines
Christian Meditation Centre
11 Osmeña Street
South Admiral Village, Bgy Merville,
Paranaque City
Metro Manila 1760
Tel: +63 2 824 9595
Fax: +63 2 823 3742
Email: Art888@info.com.ph

Singapore
Christian Meditation Centre
Church of the Holy Family
6 Chapel Road
Singapore 429509
Tel: +65 67376279
E-mail: daulet@pacific.net.sg
Tel: +65 64458062
E-mail: rebeccalim@pacific.net.sg
www.wccm.org/singapor.html

Thailand
Christian Meditation Centre
51/1 Sedsiri Road
Bangkok 10400
Tel: +66 2 271 3295
Fax: +66 2 271 2632
E-mail: sketudat@mozart.inet.co.th

United Kingdom
London Christian Meditation Centre
St Mark's
Myddelton Square
London
EC1R 1XX
Tel: +44 20 7833 9615
Fax: +44 20 7713 6346
E-mail: uk@wccm.org
www.christian-meditation.org.uk

USA
WCCM-US National Information Center
627 N 6th Avenue
Tucson
Arizona 85705-8330
Tel: +1 800 324 8305 (in the US) or +1 520 882 0290
Fax: +1 520 882 0311
E-mail: meditate@mediomedia.com
www.wccm-usa.org

Other books and teachings available through
The World Community of Christian Meditation
To order: www.mediomedia.org

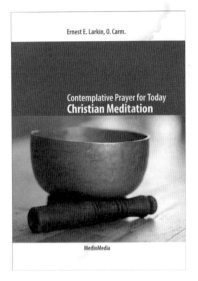

CONTEMPLATIVE PRAYER FOR TODAY:
Christian Meditation
Ernest E. Larkin, O.Carm.

Fr. Ernie has been described as a 'modern pioneer of Carmelite spirituality.' This book is the conclusion and fruit of many years of personal search, relating his own journey into Christian meditation. He brings the Carmelite tradition into dialogue with other contemporary spiritualities of the desert. Fr. Ernie's untimely death came shortly after this book was completed. The book is a legacy to us and shows the wisdom and love to which he is now fully united.

Softcover Book 152pp **#6192 £6.50 $11.95US**

Ernest Larkin (1922-2007) is best known as a beloved teacher and friend, speaking to his fellow Carmelites and the lay communities throughout the world of Carmelite spirituality. His *Spiritual Renewal of the American Priesthood* (1973) was a ground-breaking book, followed by *Silent Presence* (1981) and *Christ Within Us* (1984). From Notre Dame to Rome, Fr. Larkin's words echo within his many students and continue to influence a new generation.

Medio
Media

Published in Singapore by
MEDIO MEDIA (Publishing arm of The World Community for Christian Meditation)
www.mediomedia.org   mmi@wccm.org
THE WORLD COMMUNITY FOR CHRISTIAN MEDITATION
International Centre, St. Mark's, Myddelton Square
London EC1R 1XX, UK www.wccm.org

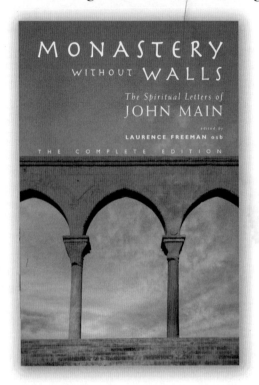